Tupperware® Cooks!

Tupperwa

re® Cooks!

Favorite Recipes of
Notable Celebrities and
World Renowned Chefs

Published by Tupperware® Brands Corporation

This book has been published in five language editions as shown below:

ISBN 0-9786455-0-2   *Tupperware® Cooks!* (English edition, 2006)
ISBN 0-9786455-1-0   *Tupperware® Cooks!* (Spanish edition, 2006)
ISBN 0-9786455-2-9   *Tupperware® Cooks!* (French edition, 2006)
ISBN 0-9786455-3-7   *Tupperware® Cooks!* (German edition, 2006)
ISBN 0-9786455-4-5   *Tupperware® Cooks!* (Japanese edition, 2006)

Contents

Introduction

Dear Reader,

It is with great pleasure that I present *Tupperware® Cooks!*, our first-ever international cookbook. This book features favorite recipes of notable celebrities and renowned chefs from around the world.

Tupperware Brands Corporation is committed to creating innovative products and concepts that demonstrate our love and appreciation for creativity and design. Thus, we are thrilled to partner with New York City's esteemed Drama Dept. in this venture.

Drama Dept. is a non-profit organization dedicated to funding and supporting affordable theater productions in New York City. In recognition of their valuable and noble efforts, Tupperware Brands Corporation has made a donation to their Production Fund.

We thank Drama Dept. for their help as our valuable partner in the creation and development of this exciting cookbook and hope that you will enjoy this copy of *Tupperware® Cooks!*

Rick Goings
Chairman and Chief Executive Officer
Tupperware Brands Corporation

Tupperware® CEO Rick Goings' Pretty's Pecan Pie

Whenever I am asked for my favorite dessert, it is an easy answer… pecan pie, and especially when my wife Susan makes it! This is her recipe … and my nickname for her has always been PRETTY… because she is.

SERVES 8

¾ **cup (6 oz/255 g) table syrup**
¾ **cup (5 oz/150 g) sugar**
¼ **cup (2 oz/60 g) butter, softened**
1 teaspoon vanilla extract (essence)
3 eggs, lightly beaten
1 cup (4 oz/120 g) chopped pecans
1 unbaked pie shell (pastry crust)

1. Preheat oven to 300°F (170°C).

2. Mix together syrup, sugar, butter and vanilla extract (essence). Fold in eggs. Gently add pecans. Pour mixture into an unbaked pie shell and place pie on a cookie sheet. Bake in preheated 300°F (170°C) oven for 1½ hours. This is great when served with a garnish of whipped cream or vanilla ice cream.

Nutrition per serving: calories 460; kilojoules 1923; protein 5g; carbohydrate 54g; total fat 26g; saturated fat 7g; monounsaturated fat 12g; cholesterol 94mg; fiber 2g.

Quick Chef
Measuring Spoons
Measuring Cups
Micro Pitcher Set
Wonderlier® Bowl Set
Saucy Silicone Spatula

"The inventive, star studded troupe that has become the last word in downtown (New York) theatrical savvy!" —*New York Times*

When we held our famous annual pot luck supper in 2005, Tupperware Brands Corporation was the exclusive sponsor and crowned the event with a Tupperware party. The event was not only our most successful ever, but produced a wonderful and ongoing relationship between Drama Dept. and Tupperware. Drama Dept. is honored to have Tupperware support our work by partnering with us on this exciting cookbook endeavor. Collecting the favorite recipes from our many important members has been an incredible project and we are thrilled to present them to you in *Tupperware® Cooks!* We hope you enjoy them as much as we do. We are "bowled" over by Tupperware's generosity and thank them for their continuing support.

Onward and upward with the arts!

Douglas Carter Beane　　　　**Michael S. Rosenberg**

Artistic Director　　　　　　　　Executive Director

www.DramaDept.org

To Market, To Market

Some of us like to dawdle in the supermarket, sampling new products, sniffing out the freshest melons, and reading labels as if they were novels. For others, getting in and out of a store quickly is top priority. No matter what your style, the key to making the trip successful is to organize.

advance planning

Keeping containers of commonly used items full or nearly full is probably the best way to prevent repeat trips to the market, so before leaving home always take a quick inventory of cupboards and see what staples—oils, flour, sugar, canned tomatoes—need replacing. Next, gather together your recipes for the week and make note of what needs to be purchased. Try to group ingredients by store sections: dairy, produce, canned goods, and fresh meats. Spending a few minutes making an organized list not only helps save time but also keeps you from shuffling up and down the same aisle, searching for that forgotten ingredient.

special ingredients

Our growing global marketplace is making it easier to buy everything from Indian curry paste to canned Italian tomatoes to imported French jam at your regular supermarket. Still, there are times you'll have to search out an authentic or gourmet item for a recipe. Take Mike Myers' cookie recipe, which calls for a British invention called custard powder, as an example. It's easy to substitute packaged instant pudding for the custard powder, but you might be curious to try his recipe with the "real" thing. Angelica Aragon's lentil recipe calls for a spice called asafetida (ah-sah-FE-teh-dah), a flavoring that comes from a fennel-like plant grown mainly in India and Iran. It's optional, and the dish tastes fine without it, but if you want to capture a more authentic flavor, it will be worth your while to go to the trouble to find the spice. But it might really be no trouble at all. Internet shops are a fast and simple way to search out specialty ingredients, or you can plan periodic shopping trips to ethnic or gourmet markets. Keep a running list of new ingredients you want to try and stock up all at once, say every two to four months. Be sure to call in advance to make sure the shop sells those ingredients.

buy fresh, buy local

As any chef will be happy to tell you, the secret to good food is top quality ingredients, so before making any recipe it pays to shop for the freshest, best ingredients you can find. With fruits and vegetables, the most flavorful produce is often what you'll find grown locally, most of the time it's easy to spot freshness and quality with just a look. Consider tomatoes, for example. Bright red ones plucked straight from the vine of a nearby farm taste amazing, while under-ripe, pink specimens (usually grown out of season and shipped long distances) have very little flavor at all.

When buying fresh seafood, local isn't always an option, unless you live near the coast, still, quality should be easy to discern. Fish, whether it is whole or cut, should smell of the sea. If it smells fishy, chances are it's been on land for too long. The smartest option is to purchase fish from a retailer who specializes in fresh seafood. Not only are these shops expert at storing fish properly, they also tend to move it in and out of the store quickly so that what you buy is more likely to be fresh. If you're buying clams for Peter and Loraine Boyle's *Linguine with Clam Sauce*, look for tightly closed shells, or shells that clamp down when tapped. When searching out shrimp (prawns) for Rocco Di Spirito's *Tangy Bianco Shrimp Salad*, look for shrimp that are firm to the touch, translucent in color, and have a mild scent. If you detect even a whiff of an ammonia odor, steer clear. That's a sure sign of spoilage.

Poultry that's been allowed to roam freely on the farm and peck at all kinds of food tends to have the best flavor. But whatever bird you buy, make sure it has no bruises and no broken skin. Poultry should smell fresh, even through the plastic wrap. As a rule, plump birds will be juicier, and younger birds, usually labeled "broilers" or "fryers," will be the tenderest.

Stocking Your Pantry

With a well-stocked cupboard and a few key items in the refrigerator, it's easy to make great meals on the spur of the moment. Keeping key staples on hand is another good way to minimize time spent at the market.

quick cooking essentials

When fresh tomatoes aren't in season, or there's not enough time to cook a fresh pot of dried beans for Famke Janssen's *Baked Beans*, canned vegetables make a fine substitute. The quality varies from brand to brand, so you'll need to try different ones to find your favorite. Most cooks agree that canned tomatoes, which are canned at the peak of freshness, are much better for sauces and soups than out-of-season tomatoes. Organic canned beans and vegetables typically have less added salt than regular varieties. Using them makes it easier to season a recipe as you cook to suit *your* tastes, without creating an overly salty flavor.

To assemble the perfect assortment of pantry staples, look at the recipes you make frequently and stock up on the ingredients they call for. Then organize your pantry so you can find whatever you need. Try putting all the Asian ingredients in one place; pasta products, rices, and starchy sides in another; and oils and vinegars for salad dressing on still another shelf.

herbs, herbs, herbs

Tossing in some chopped fresh parsley, basil, or chives can add a burst of fresh flavor to a dish and give it just the right finishing touch, one that pulls all the diverse flavors together. Fresh herbs carry more intense flavors, but dried herbs work well, too. A good rule of thumb is to substitute one teaspoon of a dried herb for each tablespoon of a fresh one. Remember that dried herbs will lose their flavor over time. Stored in Tupperware® containers, they stay fresher tasting for longer than when stored in cellophane. Still, spices that are a year old—or even older—will not carry the flavor punch of something fresh. For dried herbs and spices that you use infrequently, considering ordering small amounts online or at a local spice shop.

taking shortcuts

To save time, have some good quality, fresh convenience items like diced onions, peeled garlic, and
peeled, de-veined shrimp on hand. These partially
prepared products help cut down on the chopping,
cleaning, and prepping of ingredients and allow you
to cook up a meal in as little as half the usual time.
Another time saver is to prepare a recipe, or at least
part of a recipe, in advance. Debra Messing's
Radiatore Pasta Sauce or Lisa Rinna's *Bolognese
Sauce* can both be made on the weekend and heated up during the week as you boil a pot of pasta.
Wolfgang Puck's *Minestrone Soup*, like most soups,
tastes even better on the second or third day.

keeping it fresh

Just as important as stocking your pantry and refrigerator shelves with good
quality fresh and canned convenience items is keeping those ingredients
stored properly. Onions and potatoes are not good shelf mates (each gives off
a gas that causes the other one to spoil), so store them both in a cool, dark
place, just not the same cool, dark place. Tomatoes don't take well to refrigerator temperatures because cold air ruins their texture. For most other vegetables, storing them in the cold temperatures and humidity of your refrigerator's
produce drawer, or Tupperware® FridgeSmart® containers, is the best way to
keep them fresh. Vinegars, soy sauce and fermented foods can last indefinite-
ly, but oils will eventually become rancid, so buy them in small quantities. Olive
and vegetable oils are best when used within about six months of purchase.
Delicate nut and seed oils such as walnut or sesame oil should be stored in
the refrigerator as they spoil more quickly. If you're not certain what to put
where, or how long it will last, ask for guidelines at the grocery store.

Tips on Technique

Cooking is part art and part science. Certain standard rules always apply, but there's still room for interpretation. Call it the subjective factor; it all boils down to a matter of individual preference and taste. Many of our contributors encourage you to fill in the blanks, stirring, tasting, and creating your own food masterpiece.

get good equipment

There's a right knife (serrated) for cutting bread and tomatoes. There's a better pot (heavy-bottomed) for making the sauce for Patricia Clarkson's *Praline Parfait*. There's a perfect pan (skillet) for sautéing vegetables. That's not to say you can't cook without the right equipment. You can, but it's just a whole lot easier to put together great meals when you have the right tools. Not only do the right knives make short work of food preparation, using the right pot or pan helps when it comes to cooking food evenly. It's just possible that those sautéed vegetables or meatballs that always seem to burn are due to a poor quality skillet with a thin bottom and "hot spots" and are not a true indication of your cooking skills. If you invest in good equipment, such as Tupperware® Chef Series® cookware, it will last a lifetime.

everything in place

To take the stress out of cooking, read a recipe all the way through at least one time so you'll know what you're doing. Then, prepare each ingredient: chop the onions, measure out the oil, and pull the chicken from the refrigerator. Culinary professionals refer to this process as assembling your *mise en place*. Once ingredients are all in place, it's easy to concentrate on the task of cooking. For grilled items like Chevy Chase's lamb kabobs, each of the ingredients can be cut and prepared in advance and stored in Tupperware® containers in the refrigerator until it's time to fire up the grill.

salting to taste

Mastering the art of salting food is part technique and part individual taste. Since many of the recipes in this book don't specify amounts for salt, it's important to understand a little bit about how salt can enhance flavor. In sweet mixtures and bakery goods, salt helps to develop flavor. In bread baking, salt balances the action of yeast. Salting the water before steaming vegetables helps to season them as they cook. Most of the time, however, the key to using salt to its best advantage is to add small amounts of it as you cook a dish, which allows the food to absorb the salt and be enhanced by its flavor. Adding salt at the end of cooking is more likely to leave you with one flavor impression—salty.

frying it right

Fried foods, when cooked correctly, do not taste greasy. Both of our recipes for fried chicken — one from Ileana Douglas and one from Todd English — offer useful frying tips. If you've never fried food before, keep these general tips in mind.

- Use a deep, heavy-bottomed skillet, Dutch oven, or fryer to hold the oil.
- Let the food float rather than sit in the oil, so be generous with oil amounts.
- Add food (always at room temperature) in small batches so that the temperature of the oil stays hot. If the oil is allowed to cool even slightly, foods will absorb more of it.
- Drain fried foods on paper towels or paper bags before serving to remove excess oil.

final moments

Much as some items take well to advance preparation, there are certain foods that need last minute attention. Fresh herbs are a good example. Since they bruise and discolor easily, you'll want to chop herbs that will garnish or flavor a dish at the last minute. Toss Kyra Sedgwick's *Caesar Salad Dressing,* or any salad dressing for that matter, with greens just before serving. Delicate lettuces tend to wilt in as little as five or ten minutes if allowed to sit after being dressed.

Appetizers

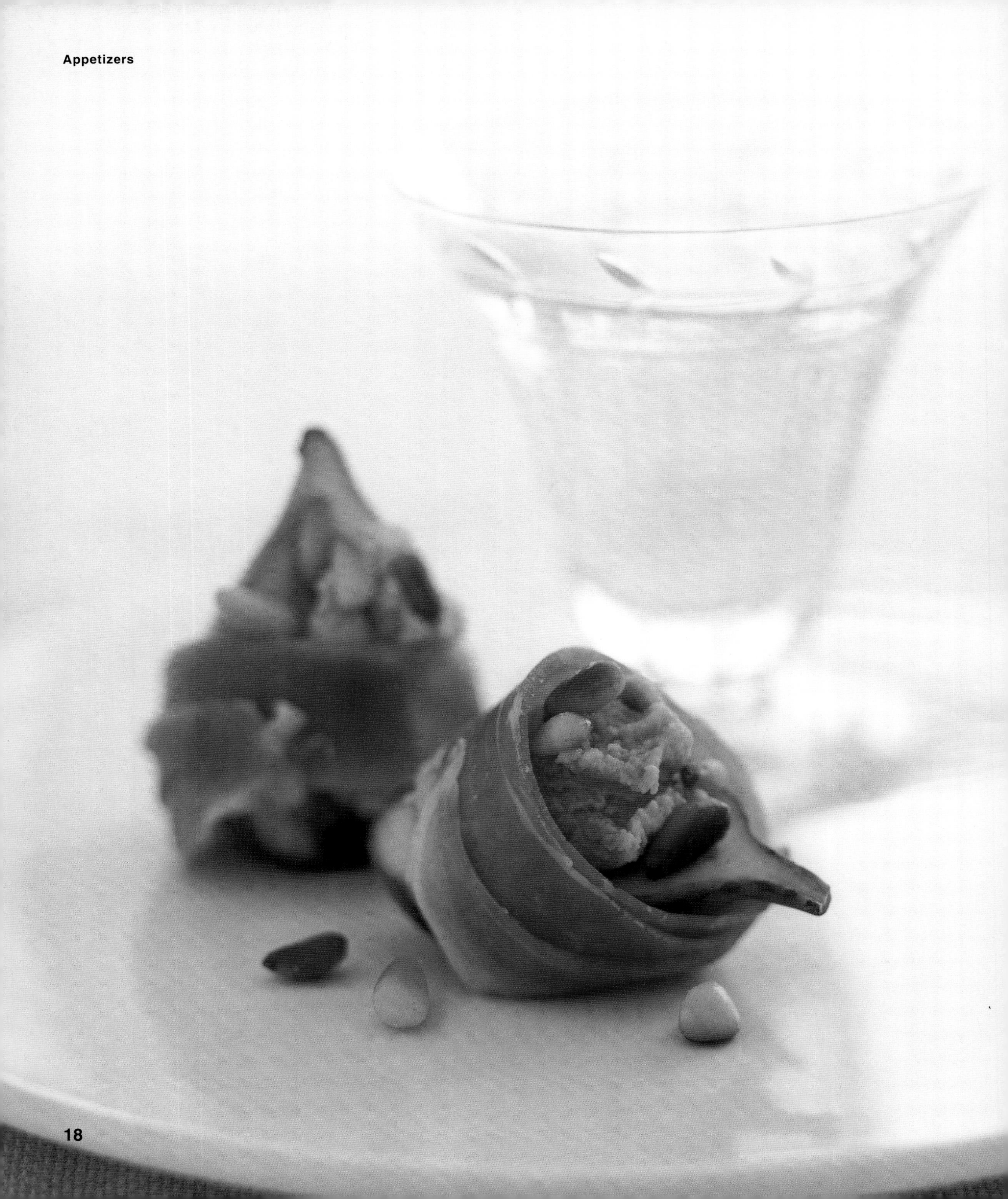

Chef Marcus Samuelsson's
Serrano Wrapped Figs With Mascarpone

A Mediterranean inspired dish, I love these flavors! It goes just as well as a starter or as a dessert. Fresh figs are in season from June through October. They may be green, white, yellowish green, or purple, depending on the variety; the purplish black Mission, the green Calimyrna, and the yellow-green Kadota are among the most popular types.

SERVES 4

½ cup pine nuts
2 tablespoons mascarpone cheese
1 teaspoon balsamic vinegar
4 ripe figs, cut in half
8 very thin slices Serrano ham or prosciutto

1. Toast pine nuts in a large skillet over medium heat for 3 to 4 minutes or until they start to turn golden brown, stirring with a wooden spoon. Watch carefully, as they can burn easily. Transfer them to a plate to cool as soon as they are done.

2. Combine the mascarpone and balsamic vinegar in a small bowl and mix well with a fork or mash with the back of a spoon. Spread ½ teaspoon of the mascarpone mixture on each fig half. Top each with a few pine nuts. Wrap each fig half in a slice of ham (the thinly sliced ham will stick to itself — no need for toothpicks). Arrange on a platter or on small plates and serve.

Tip: You can prepare the figs early in the day; cover them with plastic wrap and refrigerate. Remove from the refrigerator half an hour before serving. Ripe figs are soft, plump, and fragrant; those that have begun to shrivel slightly at the stem are at the height of ripeness and will be especially sweet. Figs are quite perishable and should be used as soon as possible, although they can be refrigerated for up to 2 days.

Nutrition per serving: calories 154; kilojoules 644; protein 9g; carbohydrate 13g; total fat 8g; saturated fat 3g; monounsaturated fat 0g; cholesterol 34mg; fiber 2g.

Chef Series™ 8" Nonstick Fry Pan

Measuring Cups

Measuring Spoons

Saucy Silicone Spatula

Prep Essentials™ Mini Mixing Bowl Set

Chef Series™ Chef's Knife

Cynthia Nixon's Tomato Surprise

For extra fun, use pepper vodka. For a LOT of extra fun, soak the tomatoes in vodka in the fridge for four to six hours and then dip them in the salt and serve.

SERVES 8–10

1 cup (8 oz/250 g) kosher salt
2 cups (11 oz/330 g) cherry tomatoes, washed and patted dry
1 cup (8 fl oz/250 ml) vodka
1 box toothpicks

1. Sprinkle salt onto individual rimmed serving plates. Divide tomatoes between small custard cups. Pour vodka into individual shot glasses.

2. To serve, give each guest a plate, custard cup and shot glass. Have guests dip tomato into vodka, then into salt. (Or, if this is too labor intensive for the guests, prepare everything in advance and put, ready-made, on serving trays.)

Nutrition per serving based on 8 servings: calories 72; kilojoules 301; protein 0g; carbohydrate 2g; total fat 1g; saturated fat 0g; monounsaturated fat 0g; cholesterol 0mg; fiber 0g.

Measuring Cups
Prep Essentials™ Measuring Cup

Cynthia Rowley's Better-Than-Bizness-Class Nuts

Spicy-sweet and a cinch to make, these nuts really take off when served warm. Use cashews, peanuts, almonds, pistachios, or whatever combination you like.

SERVES 48

2 tablespoons butter

2 tablespoons fresh sage or herb of choice, coarsely chopped

½ teaspoon cayenne pepper

2 teaspoons kosher salt

2 teaspoons dark brown sugar

3 lb (1500 g) unsalted mixed nuts

1. Preheat oven to 350°F (180°C).

2. Melt butter in a saucepan. Stir in sage, pepper, salt and sugar. Drizzle butter mixture over mixed nuts and toss to mix. Spread nuts out on a cookie sheet and bake for about 10 minutes. Watch like a hawk. They go from golden to cinders in a flash.

3. Alternatively, add nuts to spicy butter right in the pan and toast over medium-low heat until golden.

4. Drain on paper towels. Serve warm.

Nutrition per 1 oz serving: calories 173; kilojoules 723; protein 5g; carbohydrate 7g; total fat 15g; saturated fat 2g; monounsaturated fat 9g; cholesterol 1mg; fiber 3g.

Prep Essentials™ Lil' Chopper
Prep Essentials™ Large Mixing Bowl Set
Measuring Spoons
Silicone Wonder™ Mat

   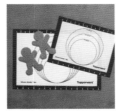

Mary Beth Peil's Yogurt Cheese

I learned how to make this from a Turkish deli owner in New Jersey (go figure). I was 5 months pregnant and totally addicted to hummus. I went there so often he showed me the fast and easy way to make my own hummus and got me hooked on olives and yogurt cheese. These days at least 2–3 times a month you will see a strainer lined with paper towel balanced over a Tupperware® container (for the liquid) sitting on my kitchen counter. When the cheese is "set," I just pour off the liquid and store the cheese in the fridge in the Tupperware® container!

1. Take a 32 oz. (1 kg) carton of good quality yogurt and empty onto large square of untreated cheesecloth (not what you use for cleaning), tie up into a pouch and hang to drip over sink or the empty yogurt container for 24 hours. (If you can't find cheesecloth, use a strainer colander with a paper towel.) After 24 hours at room temperature what you'll have is a cream cheese like substance, about one-half of the original volume.

2. Use as a substitute for sour cream, crème fraiche, or cream cheese. Mixed with minced garlic and herbes de Provence makes a low-calorie faux Boursin cheese. Use any combination of herbs (fresh or dried) to make great low-calorie dips, spreads and dressings. Fruit flavored yogurt is great on bagels and toast. Use your imagination!

Nutrition per tablespoon: calories 17; kilojoules 71; protein 1g; carbohydrate 1g; total fat 1g; saturated fat 1g; monounsaturated fat 0g; cholesterol 4mg; fiber 0g.

Prep Essentials™ Large Mixing Bowl Set
Prep Essentials™ Lil' Chopper
Saucy Silicone Spatula

Salads, Sandwiches & Soups

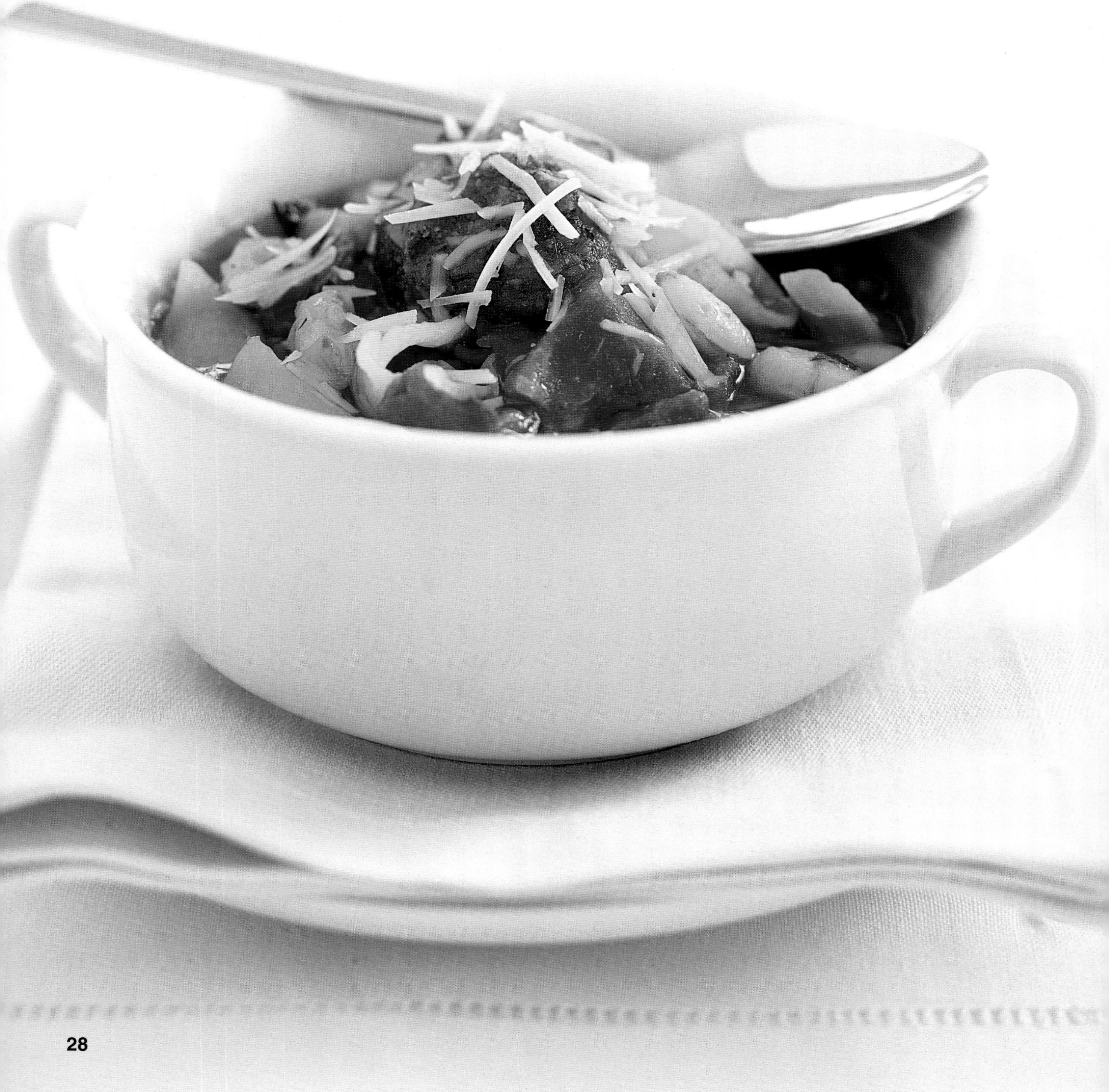

Chef Wolfgang Puck's Minestrone Soup

I consider Italy's minestrone one of the world's great soups. I love to embellish it at serving time by adding a spoonful of pesto, a drizzle of fragrant extra-virgin olive oil, or a sprinkling of high quality imported Parmesan cheese to each bowl. You could substitute canned white beans for the dried to save time. Drain the beans, rinse them, and add them with the pasta. Keep in mind, though, that the dried beans do contribute a lot of flavor to the broth. The soup will keep for 3 or 4 days in the refrigerator.

SERVES 4

SOUP:

- ½ cup (8 oz/250 g) dried great Northern white beans or navy beans
- 3 to 4 cups (750 ml to 1 L) water, or more as needed for thinning the soup
- 2 tablespoons extra-virgin olive oil
- 1 large onion, chopped
- 2 oz/60 g pancetta, chopped (optional)
- 2 large garlic cloves, minced
- 1 (28 oz/850 g) can diced tomatoes in juice
- ½ cup (2 oz/60 g) diced carrots
- 2 stalks celery, thinly sliced
- ¼ cup (¼ oz/8 g) chopped fresh spinach or parsley
- 2 small potatoes (about 6 oz/180 g), cut in small cubes
- 1 medium zucchini, halved lengthwise and cut into ½ inch (1.25 cm) pieces
- 3 sprigs fresh thyme
- Kosher salt
- Freshly ground pepper
- ½ cup (1½ oz/45 g) small dried pasta shells or elbow macaroni

FOR SERVING:

- ½ cup (2 oz/60 g) freshly grated Parmesan
- ½ cup (4 oz/125 g) prepared pesto sauce
- Extra-virgin olive oil

1. Pick through and rinse beans. Soak overnight in water, covered by 2 inches, and drain.

2. Combine with 3 cups (750 ml) of water in a 2-quart (2 L) saucepan. Bring to a boil. Reduce heat, cover, and simmer 1 hour.

3. Heat the oil in a large, heavy soup pot over medium heat. Add the onion and pancetta and cook, stirring, until the onion is tender and golden, about 5 minutes. Add the garlic and cook, stirring, for another minute until fragrant.

4. Add the tomatoes with their liquid, the beans and their broth, the carrots, celery, spinach or parsley, potatoes, zucchini, thyme, and salt and pepper to taste. Bring to a boil. Reduce heat, cover, and simmer 1 hour. Taste and adjust seasonings. The beans should be tender and the broth fragrant.

5. About 10 minutes before serving, add the pasta to the soup. If the mixture is too thick, add another cup (250 ml) of water, or more if needed. Simmer until the pasta is just tender to the bite. Adjust seasonings and serve, sprinkling each serving with freshly grated Parmesan, a spoonful of pesto, or a drizzle of extra virgin olive oil.

Recipe courtesy Wolfgang Puck, *Wolfgang Puck Makes It Easy*, Rutledge Hill Press, 2004.

Nutrition per serving: calories 361; kilojoules 1509; protein 16g; carbohydrate 44g; total fat 14g; saturated fat 4g; monounsaturated fat 6g; cholesterol 21mg; fiber 10g. (**Note:** Nutrition analysis includes Parmesan cheese garnish.)

Chef Series™ 8 Qt. Stock Pot
E-Series™ Can Opener
Grate 'N Measure™ Grater
Kitchen Duos

Fran Drescher's Simple Healthy Soup

SERVES 2

1 (10.5 oz/310 g) can tomato soup, any brand you like
5 oz (150 g) of firm or extra-firm organic tofu
1 fistful of organic baby spinach
1 tablespoon grated Parmesan cheese

1. Prepare soup according to package directions in a small saucepan.

2. Cut tofu into small cubes and add to soup. Put baby spinach on top of soup mixture and cover with lid. Cook over medium flame until soup is thoroughly heated.

3. Serve in deep bowls and sprinkle each serving with Parmesan.

Nutrition per serving: calories 226; kilojoules 945; protein 15g; carbohydrate 24g; total fat 10g; saturated fat 2g; monounsaturated fat 2g; cholesterol 4 mg; fiber 3g.

Chef Series™ 2½ Qt. Covered Nonstick Sauce Pan
Saucy Silicone Spatula
E-Series™ Can Opener
Measuring Spoons

Bryan Cranston's Spicy
Get-all-your-veggies-at-once Mexican Slaw

SERVES 8–10

2 packages Broccoli Slaw

2 cans hearts of palm, drained and cut into bite sized pieces

1 cup chopped red bell pepper

1 small can Mexican style corn—drained

1 small can sliced black olives

2 avocados in bite sized pieces

1 to 2 cups shredded cheddar cheese

2 tablespoons chopped jalapeños

1. Toss together with ranch dressing. Top with thin tortilla strips and chopped cilantro.

2. Chopped chicken can be added for main course salad.

E-Series™ Can Opener

Chef Series™ Chef's Knife

Grate 'N Measure™ Grater

Measuring Spoons

Measuring Cups

Saucy Silicone Spatula

Chef Rocco Di Spirito's Tangy Bianco Shrimp Salad With Zucchini Blossoms

Thank you for asking me to contribute. This recipe is from 5 Minute Flavor — *my latest passion. Recipes created from my home kitchen. 5 ingredients, 5 minutes to cook, insane flavor. Grab the Good Life!*

SERVES 4

1 cup (8 fl oz/250 ml) Martini & Rossi Bianco® vermouth

1½ lbs (750 g) large shrimp (prawns), peeled and deveined

Salt and pepper to taste

Juice and zest of 3 lemons

1 cup (8 oz/250 g) mayonnaise

10 large fresh zucchini (courgettes) blossoms, cut in half lengthwise

1. Bring vermouth to a boil in a large covered sauté pan over high heat. Season shrimp well with salt and pepper and add to the pan; cover. Cook, stirring occasionally, until shrimp are almost cooked through, about 2 minutes. Cool shrimp in their cooking liquid in a large bowl in the refrigerator. When cool, drain off liquid and set shrimp aside.

2. Mix together the zest of 2 lemons, all of the lemon juice, and mayonnaise in a medium bowl. Toss shrimp with sauce and season with salt and pepper.

3. To serve, arrange 5 zucchini blossom halves on each of four plates, stem ends facing inward, to form a "flower." Divide shrimp among the four plates, piling it in the center of the flower. Drizzle any remaining sauce on top of shrimp and flowers and around the plate. Evenly sprinkle the remaining zest of one lemon on the salads and serve.

Nutrition per serving: calories 636; kilojoules 2658; protein 35g; carbohydrate 9g; total fat 47g; saturated fat 1g; monounsaturated fat 0g; cholesterol 279mg; fiber 1g.

Martini & Rossi Bianco® Vermouth is a trademark of Martini & Rossi Corporation

Chef Series™ 6 Qt Nonstick Covered Sautè Pan

Measuring Cups

Prep Essentials™ Citrus Wonder™ Juicer

Prep Essentials™ Mix-N-Stor® Plus Pitcher

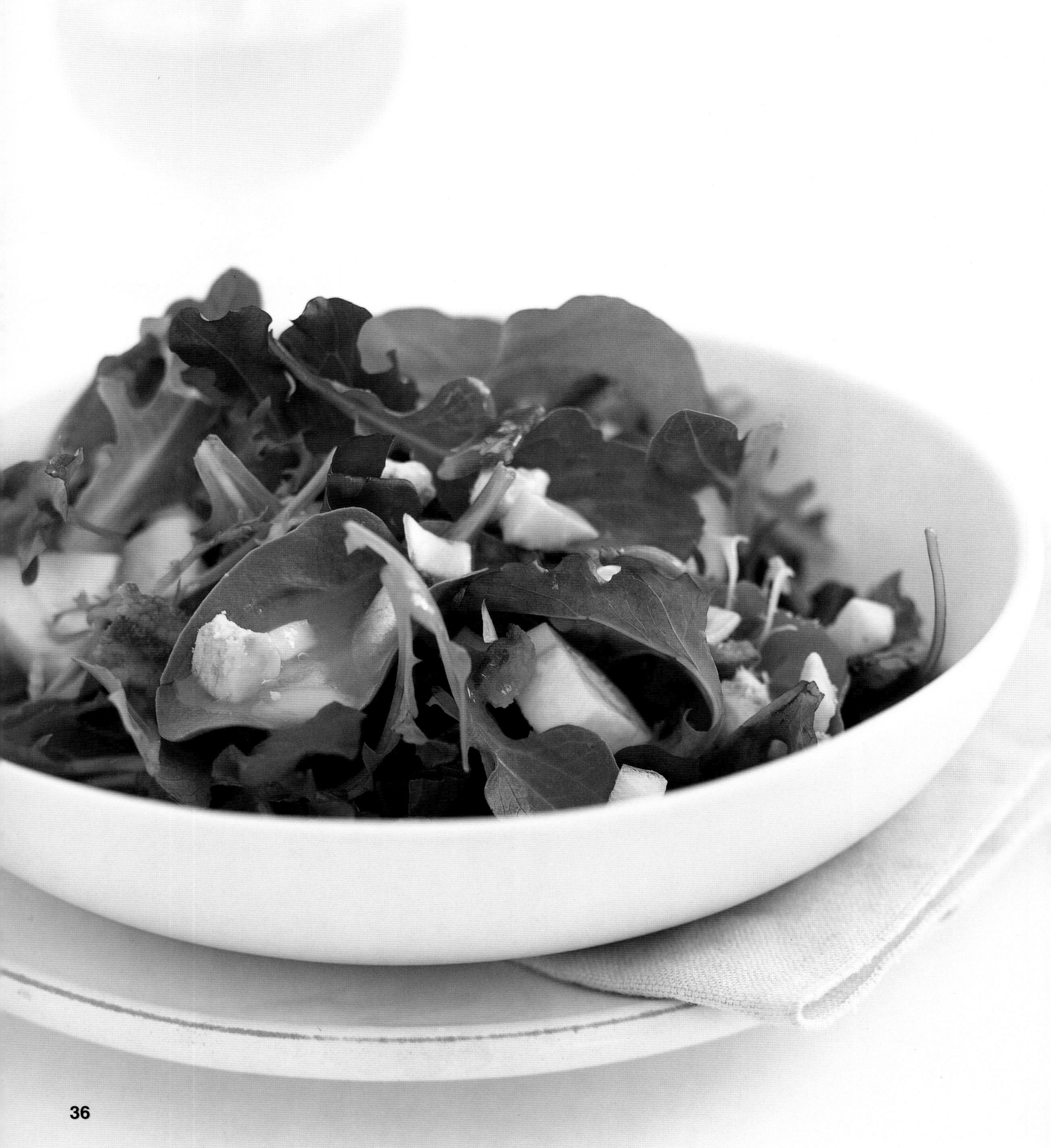

Douglas Carter Beane's Bacon Salad

Leave it to my Grandma Carter to use bacon grease and vinegar as a salad dressing. But more about her in a future play, I'm sure. This was an old family favorite at family gatherings in Tunkhannock, Pennsylvania. Imagine my surprise years later when I saw it being served in Parisian cafes.

SERVES 6

¾ lb (375 g) of chopped fresh bacon (or up to 1 lb/500 g of bacon)

1 tablespoon mild mustard

2 tablespoons apple cider vinegar

3 tablespoons honey

Salt and freshly ground pepper

1 lb (500 g) of baby greens

1 cup (5 oz/150 g) chopped Vidalia (sweet) onion

3 large hard boiled eggs, chopped

8 oz (250 g) crumbled blue cheese

1. Fry bacon until crisp. Remove bacon from pan and place on paper towel to drain. Reserve drippings and bacon.

2. Whisk mustard, vinegar, and honey into bacon drippings. Add salt (remember bacon can be salty!) and pepper to taste.

3. Toss baby greens with blue cheese, onions, chopped eggs and reserved bacon. Serve with dressing.

Nutrition per serving: calories 486; kilojoules 2031; protein 19g; carbohydrate 15g; total fat 39g; saturated fat 16g; monounsaturated fat 15g; cholesterol 173mg; fiber 2g.

Chef Series™ 8" Nonstick Fry Pan
Prep Essentials™ Lil' Chopper
Measuring Spoons
Measuring Cups

Kyra Sedgwick's Caesar Salad Dressing

SERVES 6

2 large eggs
1 tablespoon plus 2 teaspoons fresh lemon juice
1 teaspoon Worcestershire sauce
¼ teaspoon salt
⅛ teaspoon pepper
1 medium clove garlic
4 anchovy fillets, minced
⅓ cup (2.5 oz /70 g) olive oil
Fresh grated Parmesan cheese

1. Bring half a pot of water to a boil; add eggs and cook for 45 seconds. When cool, crack eggs and reserve yolks. Discard egg whites. Combine egg yolks and other ingredients, except oil and Parmesan cheese, in a small bowl and whisk until smooth.

2. Add oil in a slow stream while whisking constantly. Stir in fresh grated Parmesan cheese to complete this dressing.

Nutrition per tablespoon: calories 138; kilojoules 577; protein 2g; carbohydrate 1g; total fat 14g; saturated fat 2g; monounsaturated fat 10g; cholesterol 72mg; fiber 0g. **Note:** The nutrition analysis of this recipe includes 2 tablespoons of Parmesan.

Prep Essentials™ Mini Mixing Bowl Set
Prep Essentials™ Measuring Cup
Measuring Spoons
Chef Series™ 2½ Qt. Covered Nonstick Sauce Pan

Jane Rosenthal's Downtown Tuna Melt

When I'm feeling stressed out, nothing hits the spot like an old-fashioned Tuna Melt. It's simple and the ingredients are probably already in your kitchen.

SERVES 1

1 English muffin, toasted until crisp
1 ripe tomato, sliced
1 slice American cheese (or something more healthy)
1 (6 oz /180 g) can tuna fish, drained
Miracle Whip® salad dressing (or mayonnaise)
Dijon mustard
Pepper
Dill pickle

1. Mix tuna in a small bowl with a dollop of Miracle Whip®, a smidgen of Dijon mustard, and a sprinkle of pepper.

2. Place a scoop of tuna on top of bottom half of muffin. (Save remaining tuna for another sandwich.) Top with tomato slice and cheese, and return muffin to toaster oven. Heat for 2 minutes on "top brown" setting or until cheese melts. Top with other half of muffin. Serve on plate with a kosher dill pickle. Enjoy!

Nutrition per serving: calories 471; kilojoules 1969; protein 49g; carbohydrate 31g; total fat 15g; saturated fat 6g; monounsaturated fat 1g; cholesterol 69mg; fiber 0g.

Miracle Whip® Salad Dressing is a trademark of Kraft Foods Holdings, Inc.

E-Series™ Can Opener
Prep Essentials™ Mini Mixing Bowl Set
Saucy Silicone Spatula

Vegetables and Side Dishes

hefseries ™
by Tupperware

Dayanara Torres' Puerto Rican Mofongo

This recipe is one of my favorites not only because it's delicious but also because it reminds me of Puerto Rico. There isn't a single family gathering or holiday back home that doesn't include mofongo. It is a must!

SERVES 6

3 green plantains
1 teaspoon salt
Bacon fat, lard or vegetable oil
3 garlic cloves
1 teaspoon olive oil
½ lb (8 oz /250 g) crisp fried pork rinds
4 cups (1 L) water
Chicken broth (optional)

1. Peel plantains and cut crosswise into 1-inch (2.5 cm) slices. Soak for 15 minutes in salt and water. Drain well.

2. Heat fat or oil to 350°F (180°C) if you are using a deep fryer. Add plantain slices and fry for 15 minutes, but do not brown. Drain on paper towels.

3. In a mortar (for pounding), crush garlic cloves and sprinkle with salt; add olive oil to the mixture and keep pounding.

4. Crush a portion of the fried plantain slices and the pork rinds. Add to mortar with garlic and olive oil mixture and keep pounding. Spoon the mixture and shape into 2-inch (5 cm) balls. Repeat procedure until you use all the ingredients.

5. Place mofongo in 200°F (100°C) oven and keep warm until you are ready to serve. You can prepare chicken broth and pour over mofongo just before serving so it will be juicy.

Nutrition per serving: calories 355; kilojoules 1484; protein 24g; carbohydrate 32g; total fat 17g; saturated fat 7g; monounsaturated fat 2g; cholesterol 54mg; fiber 5g. (**Note:** Figures for fat are approximate since fried foods can absorb as little as 5% of the oil they are cooked in or much, much more. It all depends on the temperature of the oil.)

Chef Series™ 8" Nonstick Fry Pan
Measuring Cups
Measuring Spoons

Alondra de la Parra's Artichokes "La Parra" Style

Alondra de la Parra Borja, at 23, became the first Mexican woman to conduct a symphonic orchestra in New York City. De la Parra is a founding member and Artistic Director of the Philharmonic Orchestra of the Americas (Orquesta Filarmónica de las Américas) located in New York. Today, she is Main Host Director of the New Amsterdam Symphony.

SERVES 4

2.5 lb (1 kg) baby artichokes
2 tablespoons lemon juice
¼ cup (3 oz /90 gm) olive oil
1 avocado
2 tablespoons Parmesan cheese
Salt and pepper

1. Cook and peel the artichokes until only the core is left. When ready, slice cores into thin sheets. When the sheets are cut, add lemon juice freely so the artichokes do not oxidize. Add more lemon juice, as well as olive oil and avocado chopped into small pieces. Add salt and pepper; mix all ingredients.

2. Sprinkle Parmesan cheese over it and enjoy!

Nutrition per serving: calories 266; kilojoules 1112; protein 6g; carbohydrate 17g; total fat 22g; saturated fat 3g; monounsaturated fat 15g; cholesterol 2mg; fiber 10g.

Prep Essentials™ Lil' Chopper
Chef Series™ 3½" Paring Knife

Michael S. Rosenberg's Corn Pudding

My mother always said you could make vegetables taste better by adding dairy. Now, why can't I lose weight?

SERVES 6

2 large eggs
1 (17 oz /510 g) can creamed corn
1 (17 oz /510 g) can regular corn, including juice
8 oz (250 g) sour cream
½ cup (4 oz /125 g) butter
1 (8.5 oz /260 g) box corn muffin mix

1. Preheat oven to 350°F (180°C).

2. Mix all ingredients together and place in a greased baking dish. Bake uncovered at 350°F (180°C) for one hour.

Nutrition per serving: calories 513; kilojoules 2144; protein 9g; carbohydrate 57g; total fat 30g; saturated fat 16g; monounsaturated fat 10g; cholesterol 128mg; fiber 5g.

Measuring Cups
Wonderlier® Bowl Set
Saucy Silicone Spatula

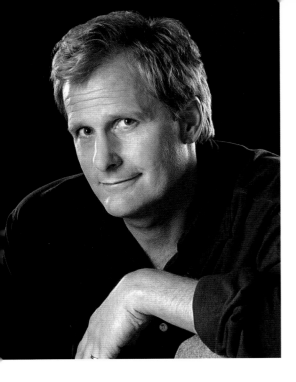

Jeff Daniels' Tomato Pudding

This recipe is courtesy of Jeff's mother, Marjorie Daniels.

SERVES 8

2 cups (2.5 oz /70 g) bread, broken into chunks
½ cup (4 oz /120 g) butter, melted
2 (28 oz /850 g) cans tomatoes
1 cup (8 oz /240 g) firmly packed brown sugar
Pinch of basil

1. Preheat oven to 350°F (180°C).

2. Combine bread and melted butter in a large bowl; let butter melt and run down into bread. Stir in tomatoes and sugar. Add a pinch of basil and spoon mixture into a baking dish. Bake at 350°F (180°C) for one hour. Mixture will be soupy in the beginning, but will thicken (and brown on top somewhat) as it bakes.

Nutrition per serving: calories 261; kilojoules 1091; protein 2g; carbohydrate 39g; total fat 12g; saturated fat 7g; monounsaturated fat 3g; cholesterol 30mg; fiber 2g.

Measuring Cups
Micro Pitcher Set
Saucy Silicone Spatula

Patrick McMullan's Green Party Potato Salad

This recipe is with special thanks to Ms. Anne.

SERVES 8–10

2 lbs (1000 g) red skinned potatoes
Salt
Black pepper
Mayonnaise
Green food coloring
4–5 chopped hard boiled eggs
Green onions (scallions)
Bacon bits (optional)

1. Boil potatoes in salted water. Let them cool; peeling is optional. Add pepper to taste.

2. Add a cup or so of mayonnaise. (A variation is a half cup of mayonnaise and a half cup of sour cream if you work out or dance a lot.) Also add a few drops of green food coloring to this mixture until you get the desired shade.

3. Add 4–5 chopped hard boiled eggs, green onions, and salt to taste. Right before serving, you can also add fresh bacon bits.

Nutrition per serving: calories 319; kilojoules 1333; protein 6g; carbohydrate 20g; total fat 24g; saturated fat 4g; monounsaturated fat 6g; cholesterol 116mg; fiber 2g.

Chef Series™ 4" Utility Knife
Saucy Silicone Spatula
Measuring Cups
Clear Impressions™ Large Bowl

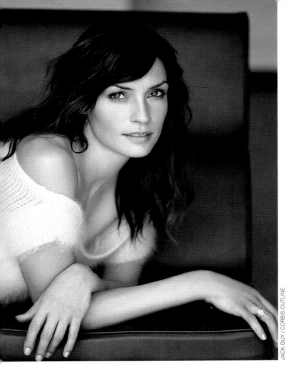

Famke Janssen's Baked Beans

Here is a Dutch recipe that I love. It uses spek, a thick Dutch bacon.

SERVES 8

4 cups (35 oz/1050 g) black or brown beans

4 oz (120g) spek/bacon, cut up into little cubes

1–2 tablespoons vinegar

¼ cup (3 oz/90 g) syrup, made from sugar beets, not from maple trees

1. Cook black or brown beans. Mix in spek. Add a splash of vinegar and pour in syrup. Add to a casserole dish and bake at 350°F (180°C) for about 45 minutes.

Nutrition per serving: calories 163; kilojoules 681; protein 7g; carbohydrate 25g; total fat 6g; saturated fat 2g; monounsaturated fat 3g; cholesterol 10mg; fiber 6g.

Measuring Cups

Chef Series™ 4" Utility Knife

Chef Series™ 6 Qt. Dutch Oven

Main Courses

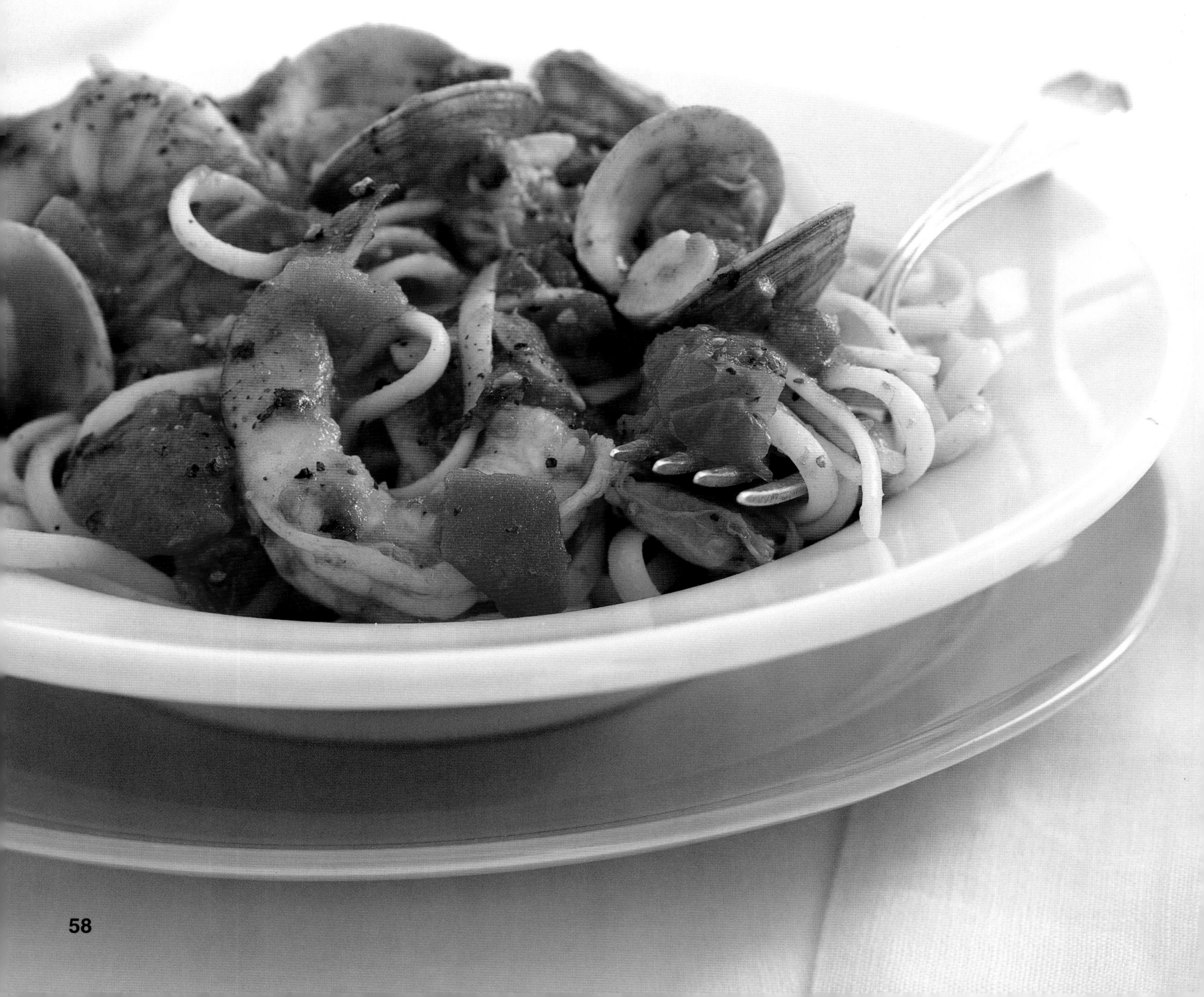

Peter and Loraine Boyle's Linguine with Clam Sauce

SERVES 4

2 tablespoons olive oil
4 cloves garlic, peeled and thinly sliced
1 (28 oz /850 g) can imported Italian plum tomatoes
1 dozen small clams, scrubbed clean
16–20 medium shrimp, peeled and deveined
1 lb (500 g) angel hair pasta or linguine

1. Heat oil in a saucepan. Add garlic and briefly sauté until tender. Stir in 2 cups of chopped imported Italian canned tomatoes. Simmer for 30 minutes.

2. Place clams (in their shells) in a small saucepan. Cover, turn on the heat and when the shells open (usually in a few minutes), remove from heat. Take clams out of shells and strain clam juice through a fine mesh strainer so that you can add it to the sauce.

3. Put shrimp into tomato sauce and let simmer. When they turn pink and are done — five minutes at most — add clam juice and shelled clams. Heat briefly until clams are warmed throughout. Add salt and pepper to taste. (If clams are very salty, you may not need to add more than a pinch of salt.)

4. Cook pasta according to package directions. Pour sauce over angel hair or linguine and serve.

   Note: For a different presentation, strain the juice as instructed but leave clams in their shells.

Nutrition per serving: calories 578; kilojoules 2416; protein 29g; carbohydrate 95g; total fat 10g; saturated fat 2g; monounsaturated fat 5g; cholesterol 56mg; fiber 5g.

Chef Series™ 4" Utility Knife
Chef Series™ 2½ Qt. Covered Nonstick Sauce Pan
Chef Series™ 6 Qt. Dutch Oven
Saucy Silicone Spatula
Measuring Spoons
Micro Pitcher Set

Michael Imperioli's Pasta Con Asparagi

SERVES 4–6

- 1½ lbs (750 g) fresh asparagus
- 3 tablespoons unsalted butter
- 2½ tablespoons olive oil
- 2 cloves garlic
- 2 cups (1 lb/500 g) canned Italian plum tomatoes, put through a sieve
- 1 tablespoon chopped fresh or 1 teaspoon dried basil
- 1 tablespoon chopped parsley
- ¾ pound (12 oz/375 g) penne or rigatoni
- 2 eggs plus 1 egg yolk, beaten well with a fork
- ½ cup (2 oz/60 g) grated Parmesan or Pecorino Romano

1. Have all the ingredients prepared and ready to go. Cut the asparagus into 2-inch (5 cm) lengths. (If the stalks are really thin, slice them in half.) Heat the butter in a skillet. Sauté the asparagus until crisp; it will brown slightly. This takes about 5 minutes.

2. Heat the olive oil, add garlic and cook until it is lightly browned; toss out the garlic. Add the tomatoes, parsley, basil and salt and pepper into the garlic flavored olive oil. Cook and stir for about 10 minutes.

3. Meanwhile put the pasta in salted boiling water and cook for 7–9 minutes.

4. Just before the pasta is done, turn off the heat under the tomatoes. Add the beaten eggs, stirring quickly so they blend in but don't scramble. (Do not boil the sauce once the eggs are mixed in.) Add the crisp asparagus to the tomato sauce turning to coat.

5. Drain the pasta, and toss it with the tomato-asparagus sauce. Stir in half the grated cheese. Save the remaining cheese to sprinkle over the top.

Nutrition per serving based on 4 servings: calories 574; kilojoules 2399; protein 20g; carbohydrate 76g; total fat 21g; saturated fat 9g; monounsaturated fat 9g; cholesterol 25mg; fiber 7g.

Chef Series™ Chef's Knife
Chef Series™ 2½ Qt. Covered Nonstick Saucepan
Chef Series™ 8 Qt. Stock Pot
Kitchen Duos
E-Series™ Can Opener

Chef Toni Mörwald's Gröstel of Sheat Fish With Garlic

SERVES 4

10 oz /300 g peeled potatoes
Oil for frying
2 red paprika (red bell peppers)
Olive oil
2 tablespoons of butter
White wine
1 cup (8 oz /250 ml) fish stock
½ cup (4 oz /125 ml) cream
Salt and pepper to taste
3 tubers (heads) garlic
1 cup (8 oz /250 ml) milk
6 (5 oz /150 g) fresh sheat fish filets
3½ oz /100 g bacon

1. Cut the peeled potatoes into small cubes (0.5 x 0.5 cm) and deep-fry them.

2. Wash the paprika (bell peppers) and cut them into rhombuses (cubes). Sweat them over low heat with oil and butter. After 3 minutes, extinguish with white wine. Then cook with soup, add the cream and more butter and strain.

3. Peel the garlic, decoct (steep) in milk about 3 minutes; strain and dry the garlic.

4. Cut the sheat fish filets into 2–3 cm (about ¾ to 1½ -inch) wide pieces, salt and pepper them and fry in olive oil and butter. At the end fry the garlic too. Swirl the paprika (bell peppers) in butter and spice with salt and pepper. Cut the bacon in slices and fry the bacon until crispy brown.

   Note: Sheat fish is found in European waters. If you can't find it, substitute a mild white fish like orange roughy or tilapia. The flavor will be slightly different.

Nutrition per serving: calories 760; kilojoules 3177; protein 55g; carbohydrate 29g; total fat 46g; saturated fat 17g; monounsaturated fat 19g; cholesterol 226mg; fiber 3g. (**Note:** Figures for fat are approximate since fried foods can absorb as little as 5% of the oil they are cooked in or much, much more. It all depends on the temperature of the oil.)

Chef Series™ 4 Qt. Covered Nonstick Sauce Pan
Chef Series™ 8" Nonstick Fry Pan
Vertical Peeler

Japan's Iron Chef Mr. Michiba's Kaisen Nikogori

A beautiful terrine of Japanese seafood delicacies which will delight your guests. Terret is a professional setting ingredient. You can substitute the same amount of solid Japanese agar-agar as an alternative.

SERVES 8–10

2½ oz (80 g) mild white fish
Soy sauce
Mirin (Japanese sweet sake)
1¼ cups (600 ml) bonita soup
2½ oz (80 g) trepang (dried sea cucumber)
2½ oz (80 g) King Crab meat
1 oz (30 g) dried scallops
1¼ oz (40 g) dried shitake mushrooms
Sugar
5 miso preserved egg yolks
1¼ oz (40 g) miso preserved cream cheese
1¼ oz (40 g) broccoli
¾ oz (20 g) yurine (lilly root)
Vinegar
1½ oz (50 g) carrot
8 oz (250 g) yamato yam
2 terret
Gold leaf

1. To prepare the filling, cut the fish into bite size pieces. Season with a little of the bonito soup, soy sauce, and mirin. Soften trepang. Cut it into bite size pieces and season with a little of the bonito soup, soy sauce and mirin. Cut the King Crab into ¾-inch (2 cm) portions. Place the dried scallops with the bonita soup and soy sauce.

2. Place the dried shitake mushrooms in another bowl and cover with water to soak. Season with soy sauce and sugar.

3. Prepare the miso preserved boiled egg yolks and cream cheese.

4. Cut broccoli into bite size pieces and blanch in salted water.

5. Break yurine (lilly root) into flakes and boil until soft with salt and vinegar.

6. Cut carrot into desired shapes and blanch in salted water.

7. Puree yam.

8. Heat terret with bonita soup over medium heat until the terret is dissolved. Add the pureed yam and stir until combined. Pour some of the yam mixture into a silicon loaf baking form. Neatly arrange the other ingredients (fillings) and cover with the remaining yam mixture. Refrigerate until set.

9. Remove terrine from silicon form. Cut into desired shapes and arrange in a Gift Zen. Decorate with some of the gold leaf.

Nutrition per serving: calories 187; kilojoules 782; protein 14g; carbohydrate 17g; total fat 6g; saturated fat 2g; monounsaturated fat 2g; cholesterol 160mg; fiber 1g.

Prep Essentials™ Measuring Cup
Prep Essentials™ Mini Mixing Bowl Set
Easy–Lift™ Cutting Board
Chef Series™ Chef's Knife

Ralf Moeller's Cabbage Roulades

SERVES 4

1 head of Savoy cabbage
1 large onion
7 oz (200 g) smoked slab bacon, half of it sliced and half of it diced
7 oz (200 g) diced potato
3½ oz (100 g) walnuts
7 oz (200 g) carrots
7 oz (200 g) parsnip root
5 oz (150 g) heavy cream
Nutmeg
Sugar
Butter
Instant vegetable broth (consommé)
2 teaspoons chopped flat leaf parsley

1. Preheat oven to 350°F (180°C).

2. Blanch 8 Savoy cabbage leaves in salted water. Dice the remaining cabbage, sauté it lightly with the onion and season to taste. Add diced bacon and sauté.

3. Fry diced potato in fat, add to the cabbage-onion mixture and fold in the heavy cream, nutmeg and sugar. Place two strips of bacon in a large ladle, crossed, place a cabbage leaf on top, with the edges extended over the ladle. Place the sautéed vegetables on top and close it by folding. Then turn roulade upside down.

4. Peel carrot and parsnip root, slice thinly and sauté in butter. Add instant broth and water. Place the roulades on top and cook in the pre-heated oven at 350°F (180°C) for 14–18 minutes. Baste with the juices. Before serving, top with the chopped parsley.

Nutrition per serving: calories 677; kilojoules 2830; protein 15g; carbohydrate 37g; total fat 55g; saturated fat 19g; monounsaturated fat 17g; cholesterol 90mg; fiber 9g. **Note:** Nutrition analysis is based on using 1 tablespoon butter and 1 teaspoon sugar.

Easy–Lift™ Cutting Board
Chef Series™ 8" Nonstick Fry Pan
Chef Series™ 8 Qt. Stock Pot
Measuring Spoons

Michael Brandner's Tagliatelle With Vodka

SERVES 4–6

4–5 white onions
Instant vegetable broth (consommé)
Juniper berries
Bouquet garni
1 lb (500 g) tagliatelle
2 tablespoons heavy cream
Olive oil
Bay leaves
Salt
1 teaspoon sugar
½ ring spicy Italian salami, cut into thin slices
10–12 cherry tomatoes, rinsed and dried
2½ –3 oz (80 –100 ml) vodka
1 bunch flat leaf parsley
Black pepper

1. Peel onions and cut into thin slices.

2. Boil water in a pasta pot, adding a few teaspoons of the instant broth, the juniper berries, and bouquet garni. Cook the pasta *al dente*.

3. Heat the olive oil in a saucepan and sauté the onion rings with the bay leaves and juniper berries. Add a pinch of salt and 1 teaspoon sugar. Add the salami slices and fry. Add the tomatoes and when they have softened, fold in the heavy cream. Pour the vodka into a flat ladle and when it's hot, light it and add it while it's burning to the sauce. Drain the pasta and add to the pan. Serve with flat-leaf parsley and black pepper.

Nutrition per serving: calories 777; kilojoules 3248; protein 24g; carbohydrate 104g; total fat 25g; saturated fat 7g; monounsaturated fat 14g; cholesterol 33mg; fiber 7g. **Note:** Nutrition analysis is based on using 3 tablespoons oil and 4 oz (120g) salami.

Chef Series™ 8 Qt. Stock Pot
Chef Series™ 4 Qt. Covered Nonstick Sauce Pan
Measuring Spoons
Prep Essentials™ Measuring Cup

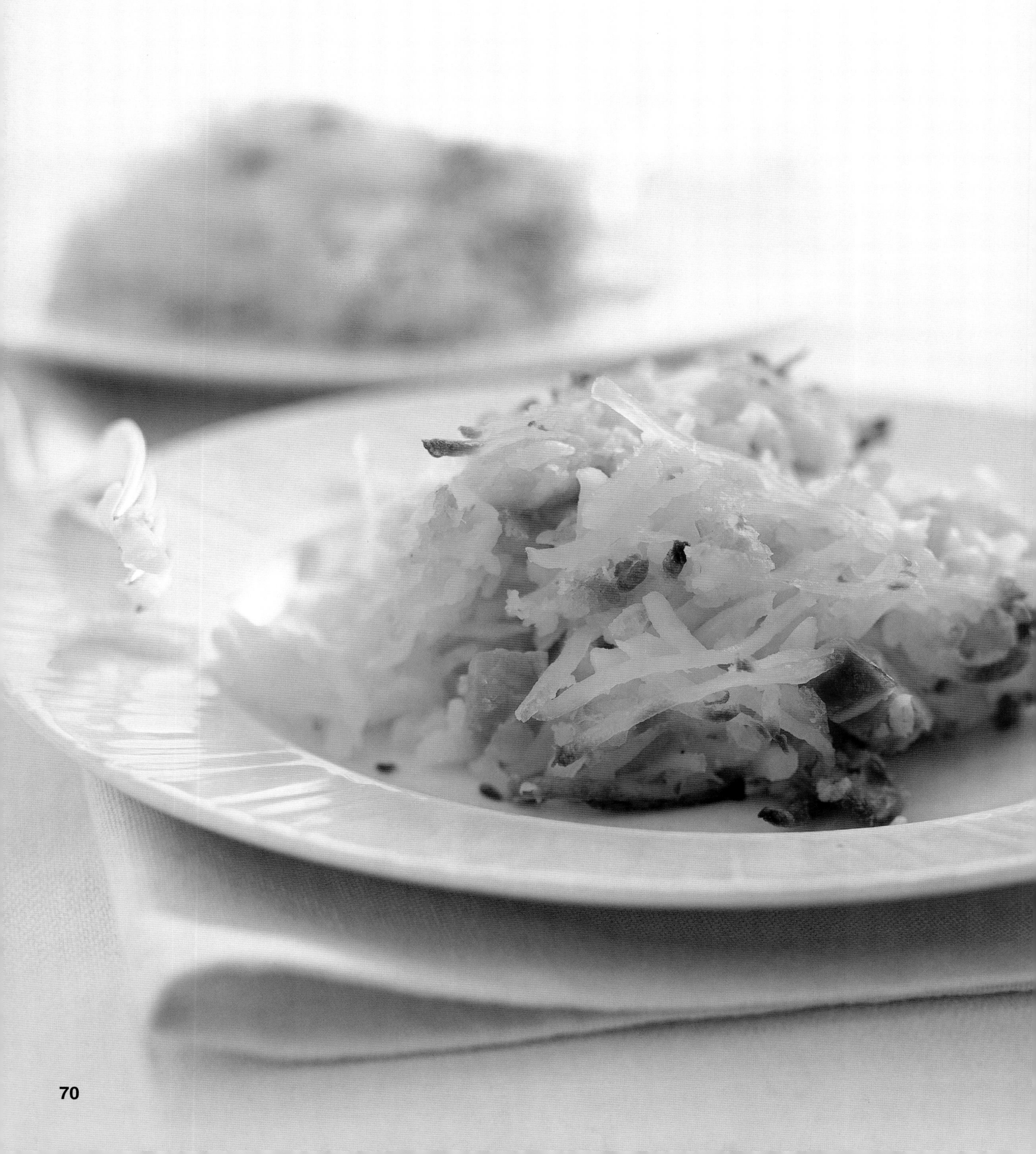

Eva Padberg's Backskloss Baked Dumpling

The word "backskloss" stems from the word "backs" meaning baking house, where this dish was baked in former times.

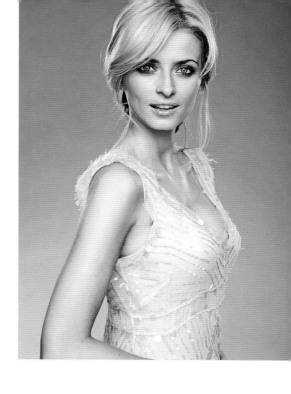

SERVES 5

- **1 bread roll (French or Kaiser)**
- **4½ lbs (2 kg) potatoes**
- **1½ lbs (750 g) smoked pork chops, diced**
- **1 lb (500 g) sauerkraut**
- **Salt**
- **Oil**

1. Soak the bread roll in water until soft; squeeze out excess water.

2. Grate the peeled raw potatoes, season with salt. Then add bread to the grated potato.

3. Layer the sauerkraut, the diced meat and the potato in a casserole dish, finishing with a layer of potato. Drizzle generously with oil and bake in oven at moderate heat for two hours or until golden brown.

Nutrition per serving: calories 798; kilojoules 3336; protein 40g; carbohydrate 81g; total fat 41g; saturated fat 12g; monounsaturated fat 19g; cholesterol 79mg; fiber 12g. **Note:** Nutrition analysis is based on using ½ cup (2 oz /60 g) oil.

Prep Essentials™ Large Mixing Bowl Set

Grate 'N Measure™ Grater

Chef Series™ 6 Qt. Covered Nonstick Sauté Pan

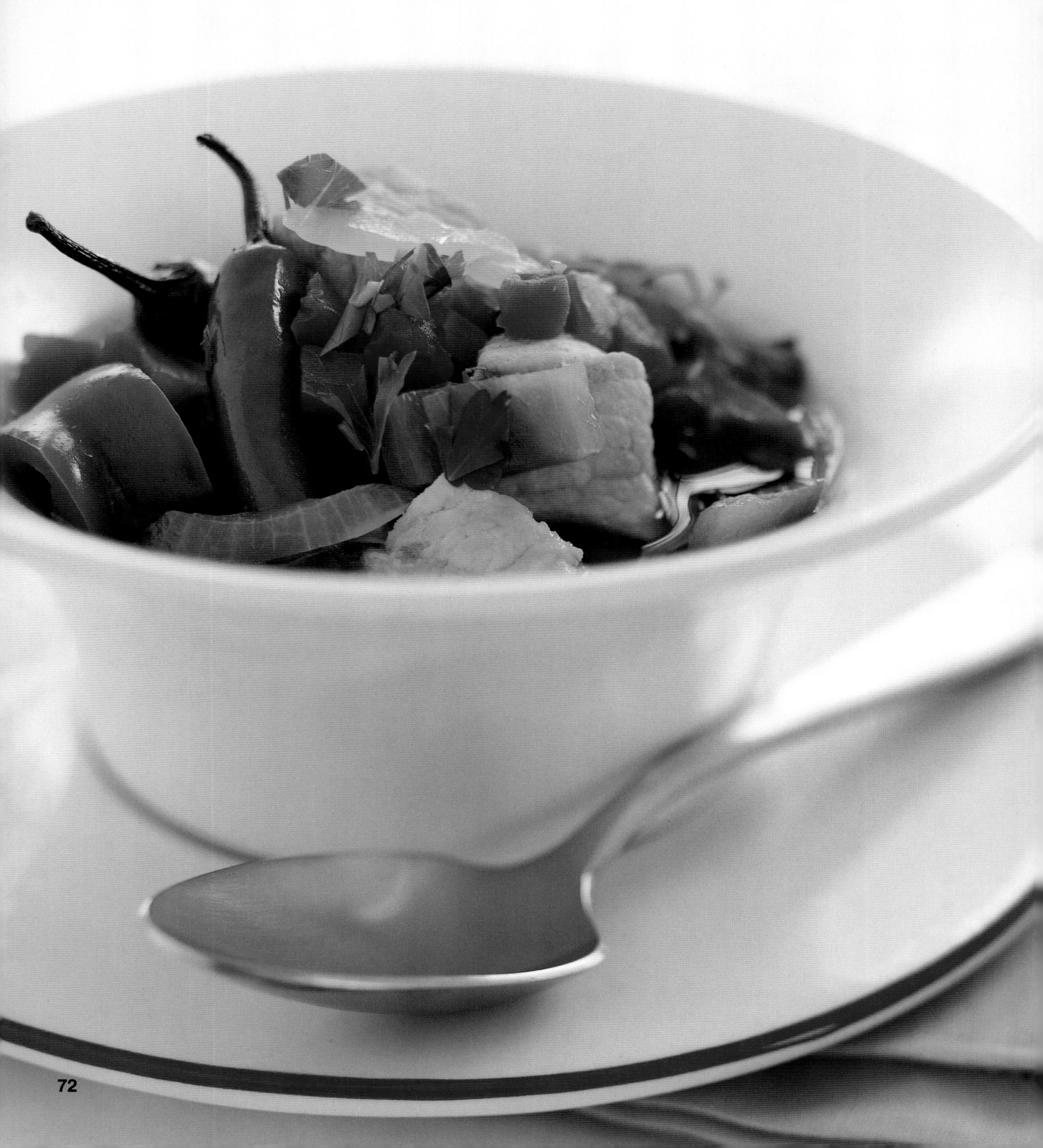

Pedro Diego Alvarado's Pork Meat in Pulque

Pedro Diego Alvarado is the grandson of Diego Rivera. After studying in Mexico and Paris, his specialty is to paint still life. It is a mighty Mexican nature that shows through not only in his finished work, but also in his personal exalted vision. From 1993 to 2000, he was part of the Artistic Creators National System, and has participated in several art exhibits in Mexico, New York, Chicago, and Paris.

A spiritual drink consumed in Mexico, pulque is obtained by fermenting "aguamiel," or juice obtained from the "maguey" trunk or hedge, before it blooms. If that's not available, the pork can also be cooked in beer.

SERVES 8

3⅓ lbs (1.5 kg) of pork loin
Salt
2 spoonfuls lard or corn oil
2 onions, peeled and chopped
3⅓ lbs (1.5 kg) tomatoes, seeded, peeled and chopped
8 serrano peppers, chopped or left whole
1 teaspoon sweet marjoram
10 big peppers (capsicum)
¼ cup (½ oz/15 g) chopped parsley
2 little pieces of (stick) cinnamon
4 cups (1 qt/1 L) pulque or beer
Salt
1 teaspoon of sugar

1. Chop pork meat into pieces; boil in salted water.

2. Heat the lard separately; add onions and fry until they are clear. Add tomatoes, serrano peppers, sweet marjoram, peppers, parsley, cinnamon, pulque (or beer), sugar, and salt to taste. Cook for 25 minutes over a slow fire. (They are perfectly seasoned now) Then add pork and sugar and cook for a long time (up to 1 hour) over a slow fire until sauce is seasoned and thick.

Nutrition per serving: calories 502; kilojoules 2098; protein 42g; carbohydrate 25g; total fat 23g; saturated fat 9g; monounsaturated fat 10g; cholesterol 116mg; fiber 7g.

Measuring Spoons
Measuring Cups
Micro Pitcher Set
Quick Chef
Chef Series™ Chef's Knife
Chef Series™ 8 Qt. Stock Pot

Angélica Aragón's Lentils

Angélica Aragón is a Mexican actress who has worked in theater, cinema, and television for more than thirty years. She has worked with directors such as Alfonso Arau, Jorge Fons among many others and performed with Woody Allen, Sharon Stone, Gael García, and Diego Luna.

This Bengali dish is easy to digest so it is recommended for children, elderly people, or convalescents. Serve it on a bland rice bed ornamented with coriander leaves and fine green chile de árbol slices. Add natural yogurt and try to eat the dish with the fingers of your right hand as is the traditional custom in India.

SERVES 4–6

1 cup lentils or peas without peel
8 cups (2 qt/2 L) cold water
1 teaspoonful ground cumin
1 teaspoonful ground coriander
1 teaspoonful asafetida (optional)
3 bay (laurel) leaves, fresh or dry
3 pods cardamom, green or black
2 teaspoons vegetable oil
1 dry chile de árbol (tree pepper)
1 teaspoon cumin seed
½ onion, finely chopped
3 cloves garlic, chopped
1 teaspoon chopped ginger
2 teaspoons butter
1 cup (8 fl oz/250 ml) fresh or canned coconut milk
2 teaspoons salt
1 teaspoon sugar
½ teaspoon ground black pepper
Fresh cilantro (coriander) leaves
1 fresh green chile de árbol, seeded and cut into long slices

1. Wash and rinse lentils three times and put into a big pot. Add water, ground cumin, coriander, asafetida, and bay leaves. Open cardamom pods and stir seeds into pot. Put pot over a high fire (heat) and let it boil for 20 minutes. Clear away any foam that forms on the surface.

2. Fry the chile de árbol and the cumin seed separately in hot oil in a frying pan or a big casserole. Add onion and cook until clear. Stir in garlic, ginger, and butter; fry them, stirring frequently.

3. When lentils grow soft, add coconut milk, salt, and sugar and bring to a boil again. Add the fried onion mixture and all the excess oil and butter. Reduce the fire (heat) to the minimum. Stir in the pepper. Let simmer for 10 minutes, or until it thickens. Serve with fresh cilantro leaves and chile.

Nutrition per serving: calories 343; kilojoules 1434; protein 16g; carbohydrate 35g; total fat 17g; saturated fat 12g; monounsaturated fat 2g; cholesterol 5mg; fiber 17g.

Measuring Spoons
Chef Series™ 9½" Covered Nonstick Fry Pan
Chef Series™ 8 Qt. Stock Pot
Saucy Silicone Spatula
Kitchen Duos

Carleton Varney's Draper's Cafe Chicken Pot Pie

This homey dish — perfect for lunch or a light supper — was a favorite of Dorothy Draper, and is featured in her namesake cafe at the Greenbrier Hotel. Unlike a traditional "pot pie," in this recipe the pastry crust is baked separately so it stays flaky and crisp.

SERVES 8

1 (3 lb/1500 g) chicken
4 tablespoons unsalted butter
1 cup diced carrots
1 cup sliced celery
1 cup diced onion
1 cup quartered button mushrooms, about 2 oz (60 g)
Salt & freshly ground black pepper, to taste
6 tablespoons all-purpose (plain) flour
½ cup (4 fl oz/125 ml) dry white wine
3 cups (24 fl oz/750 ml) chicken stock
1 cup (8 oz/250 ml) half-and-half or light cream
1 lb (500 g) homemade or prepared frozen puff pastry, thawed

1. Put the chicken in a stock pot with lightly salted cold water to cover. Bring to a boil, reduce the heat and poach gently, skimming frequently, until the chicken is very tender when pierced with a knife, approximately 45–55 minutes. Leave to cool in the poaching liquid. When cool enough to handle, remove all the meat, using a paring knife and your fingers. Discard any skin, fat, or gristle. Cut the meat into 1-inch dice. (Note: the poaching liquid can be used as the chicken stock. Reduce the stock by boiling it down if necessary to ensure a full flavor.)

2. In a large heavy-bottomed saucepan, heat half the butter over medium heat and sauté the carrots, celery, and onion until they are beginning to soften, about 5–7 minutes. Add the mushrooms and continue cooking until their liquid has been rendered and evaporated, about 3–4 minutes. Season to taste with salt and pepper.

3. Add the remaining butter and stir until melted. Then sprinkle the flour over the vegetables. Cook, stirring constantly for about 2 minutes. Add the white wine. Stir to dissolve any lumps of flour; then add the chicken stock and stir until combined. Reduce the heat and simmer until the vegetables are very tender and the sauce has thickened, about 15 more minutes. Add the half-and-half and bring to a boil. Add the chopped chicken, cook for a few more minutes to heat through. Season to taste with salt and pepper.

4. Preheat the oven to 400°F (200°C).

5. Roll out the puff pastry ⅛-inch (0.3 cm) thick and cut out 8 circles the same diameter as the serving bowls. Place the pastry circles on an ungreased baking sheet and prick the entire surface with the tines of a fork. (The pastry circles should be flaky but not risen too high.) Bake at 400°F (200°C) until deep golden brown and slightly puffed, about 20 minutes.

6. To serve, divide the hot chicken mixture between the 8 serving bowls and top with a puff pastry circle.

Nutrition per serving: calories 557; kilojoules 2328; protein 27g; carbohydrate 45g; total fat 30g; saturated fat 11g; monounsaturated fat 13g; cholesterol 88mg; fiber 5g.

Chef Series™ 8 Qt. Stock Pot
Chef Series™ 4 Qt. Covered Nonstick Sauce Pan
Measuring Cups
Measuring Spoons
Quick Chef

Chef Sara Moulton's Chicken with Sausage and Hot Cherry Peppers

This is based on an Italian dish called scarpariello—sort of a "turf and turf." I love the combination of chicken and sausages to begin with, and when you throw in the pickled peppers, the whole dish takes on a lively peppery taste. If you are a glutton for very spicy food, use hot Italian sausage. If you are trying to cut back on the fat, use turkey sausages. Serve with Mediterranean Orzo Pilaf or buttered noodles.

SERVES 4

4 chicken breast halves, with skin and bone, halved crosswise
Kosher salt and freshly milled black pepper
2 tablespoons extra virgin olive oil
½ lb (250 g) sweet or hot Italian sausage, cut into ½-inch (1.25 cm) pieces
4 pickled cherry peppers (capsicum), quartered, stems and seeds discarded
2 garlic cloves, minced (about 2 teaspoons)
1 cup (8 fl oz/250 ml) white wine
1 (14 oz/430 ml) can chicken broth or 1¾ cups chicken stock
2 (6½ oz/195 g) jars marinated artichoke hearts, drained
1½ tablespoons unbleached all-purpose (plain) flour

1. Preheat the oven to 350°F (180°C).

2. Season the chicken on all sides with salt and pepper. Heat the oil in a large skillet over high heat until hot. Reduce the heat to medium-high and add the chicken to the skillet, skin side down. Sauté until nicely browned, about 10 minutes. Place the chicken, skin side up, on a rimmed baking sheet. Bake in the center of the oven 25 minutes or until just cooked through.

3. Meanwhile, add the sausage to the skillet in which you cooked the chicken. Cook over medium-high heat until lightly browned, about 8 minutes. Add the peppers and garlic; cook for 1 minute. Add the wine and broth and cook until reduced by half, about 5 minutes. Stir in artichoke hearts.

4. Whisk together 2 tablespoons of water and the flour; whisk into the sausage mixture and cook until thickened. Transfer the chicken to a serving platter; cover loosely with aluminum foil, and let rest 5 minutes. Stir any juices that have collected on the baking sheet into the sauce. Return the sauce to a boil and spoon over the chicken.

Nutrition per serving: calories 556; kilojoules 2324; protein 44g; carbohydrate 16g; total fat 34g; saturated fat 8g; monounsaturated fat 14g; cholesterol 116mg; fiber 4g.

Chef Series™ 9½" Covered Nonstick Fry Pan
Prep Essentials™ Lil' Chopper
Measuring Cups
Measuring Spoons
Kitchen Duos

Sarah Jessica Parker's Roasted Chicken

This recipe was given to me by friends. I have no knowledge of the origins. I'm not claiming for one minute that it's an original recipe. Just so everyone is clear.

SERVES 4–6

1 (4 lb/2000 g) chicken

DRY RUB:
Kosher salt
Cayenne pepper
Crushed fennel seed

1. Preheat oven to 400°F (200°C).

2. Remove giblets and parts from interior of the chicken; discard or save for another use.

3. Thoroughly wash and pat dry the whole chicken. Generously rub the interior of the chicken with kosher salt.

4. To make dry rub, combine equal parts of salt, cayenne pepper and crushed fennel seed. Cover the outside of the chicken, bottom side first, with dry rub. Rest the chicken, breast side up, on a "V" shaped rack and place rack in a roasting pan. Roast on middle shelf of oven for 1 hour and 12 minutes. (It needs no basting.) Enjoy!

Nutrition per serving based on 4 servings: calories 461; kilojoules 1927; protein 39g; carbohydrate 3g; total fat 32g; saturated fat 9g; monounsaturated fat 12g; cholesterol 129mg; fiber 2g.

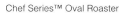

Chef Series™ Oval Roaster

B. D. Wong's "General Gong's Chicken"

General Gong Fei was my character's name in "Shanghai Moon" at Drama Dept. This is a real basic Chinese chicken recipe. I am still learning how to cook, and I am in the mood these days of making everything as easy as possible. I have just taken my mom's recipe and kind of "bachelorized" it. I was going to call it "B.D. Wong Bastardizes his Mom's Chicken" but that didn't sound quite as elegant as I'd hoped. Oh, I forgot to tell you that if you like real specific recipes, this one might make you want to set yourself ablaze.

Chicken
Low sodium soy sauce
Garlic
Ginger
Honey

1. Basically you get some chicken. You can get a whole, cut-up chicken, or just pick your favorite parts and get a "coupla few" pounds. (This is really good with chicken wings, for parties and stuff, and any other combo of parts for BBQs, picnics and parties.)

2. You get whatever amount of chicken you want to make, and then you wash it and paper towel it dry and do whatever your mom taught you to do, and then you put it in a big Tupperware container. (Really, this is part of the recipe. Use an old one from your mom's stash, the kind that burps real good.) Then you take a bottle of low sodium soy sauce, and just pour it over the chicken until it's just mostly covering all the chicken. Then take a few cloves of garlic, let's just say one clove for every three pieces of chicken, and smash them by covering them with a big knife and pounding the blade down with your fist hard. Take the "road kill" garlic and sprinkle it all over the top. Then mince up some ginger. I would say about the same amount as the garlic. One thumb size piece of ginger is about two cloves, wouldn't you say? Sprinkle that over the top of the chicken/soy sauce/garlic mess as well. Then take a few tablespoons of honey — let's say a tablespoon per two pounds of chicken — and drizzle that over the top. Then all you do is put the top on the container, burp it, shake it around to get the honey and other stuff dispersed. Put it in the refrigerator upside down overnight.

3. When you're ready to make chicken, preheat the oven to 350°F (180°C).

4. Put the chicken on a big broiling pan, skin side down, for a half hour. Then turn each piece and bake for another half hour.

   Tip: You could also marinate the chicken in a shallow oven tempered glass baking dish, cover it with plastic wrap and refrigerate. Then just remove the wrap and bake the whole thing for an hour, marinade and everything, turning the chicken pieces so they are not all submerged the whole time. This is also nice if you don't have overnight to put the chicken in the fridge. Then you have a kind of hot soy sauce marinade that is nice.

Nutrition per serving: calories 446; kilojoules 1864; protein 47g; carbohydrate 12g; total fat 22g; saturated fat 6g; monounsaturated fat 9g; cholesterol 142mg; fiber 0g. **Note:** Nutrition analyis is based on using a 3 lb (1.5 kg) chicken for 4 servings.

Prep Essentials™ Mini Mixing Bowl Set
Measuring Spoons
Saucy Silicone Spatula
Chef Series™ 4" Utility Knife
Season-Serve® Container

Chef Todd English's Southern Fried Chicken

SERVES 4–6

CHICKEN:

5 lbs (2500 g) lard

1 lb (500 g) smoked slab bacon

1 quart (32 oz/1 L) buttermilk

1 cup (2 oz/60 g) chopped parsley

1 (3 lb/1500 g) roaster chicken, hacked into 8 pieces

2–3 cups (10–14 oz/310–465 g) all-purpose (plain) flour

1 tablespoon Hungarian paprika

2 teaspoons kosher salt

2–3 teaspoons freshly ground black pepper

2 teaspoons cayenne pepper

1 tablespoon kosher salt

2–3 teaspoons freshly ground black pepper

GRAVY:

Reserved slab bacon, cut into ½ inch (1.25 cm) cubes

2 tablespoons butter

1 cup (5 oz/150 g) chopped onion

1 cup (8 fl oz/250 ml) bourbon

2 tablespoons flour

4 cups (32 oz/1 L) chicken stock

2–3 tablespoons chopped fresh parsley for garnish

1. Melt lard in a large and deep cast iron skillet and simmer bacon in the lard for 30–40 minutes. Remove bacon from lard, drain and set aside.

2. In a mixing bowl, combine buttermilk, parsley and chicken. In a separate bowl, combine flour, paprika, 2 teaspoons salt, black pepper, and cayenne. Remove chicken from milk and dredge in flour mixture for a generous coating. Place back in milk, then back in flour.

3. Add chicken to the lard and fry in a gentle "rolling" boil for 15–20 minutes. Turn chicken and fry 12–15 minutes on the other side.

4. Remove chicken from pan with a slotted spoon and drain on paper towels. Season with remaining 1 tablespoon salt and 2–3 teaspoons pepper.

5. While chicken is frying, prepare gravy. Slice fatty top off cooked slab bacon and set aside.

6. Melt butter in a medium sized saucepan over medium high heat. Sauté onions until they begin to turn clear. Add bacon and bourbon and cook 2–3 minutes. Add flour, stir together and cook 4–5 minutes.

7. In a separate saucepan, heat chicken stock. In 2–3 tablespoon batches, whisk bacon roux into chicken stock. Simmer to reduce by half, about 15 minutes.

To Plate: Place chicken pieces on a serving platter. Spoon gravy over top. Slice reserved crisped bacon fat and scatter on top.

Nutrition per serving based on 4 servings: calories 1543; kilojoules 6450; protein 69g; carbohydrate 53g; total fat 102g; saturated fat 38g; monounsaturated fat 43g; cholesterol 263mg; fiber 3g. (**Note:** Figures for fat are approximate since fried foods can absorb as little as 5% of the oil they are cooked in or much, much more. It all depends on the temperature of the oil.)

Kitchen Duos
Wonderlier® Bowl Set
Chef Series™ 8" Nonstick Fry Pan
Prep Essentials™ Lil' Chopper
Chef Series™ 4" Utility Knife

Ileanna Douglas' Fried Chicken

SERVES 4–6

1 whole chicken
Salt and pepper
Old Bay® seasoning
Seasoned salt
All-purpose (plain) flour
Canola oil

1. I think the secret to fried chicken is to first cut up a whole chicken into pieces. Then wash and dry pieces but leave them damp. I season the chicken with salt, pepper, Old Bay® seasoning and Season All® seasoned salt. (I also put seasoning in the flour.) Then flour all the pieces and set aside.

2. Use a large, heavy skillet. Fill the skillet ¼–½ inch with oil. I prefer canola oil because it has no taste. Make sure the oil is very hot. Carefully place the chicken pieces in skin side down. I prefer doing thighs and legs first, then breasts.

3. Now this is very IMPORTANT, as a true southern Louisiana woman taught me, and it is foolproof. It's all in the cooking. Cook chicken 6 minutes uncovered; cover and cook 9 minutes. Do not touch the chicken during these 15 minutes. Then uncover and flip, and again cook 6 minutes uncovered and 9 minutes covered. At this point, you may need to cook the legs a little longer. Place cooked pieces on rack for 15 minutes. Then serve and enjoy!

Nutrition per serving based on 4 servings: calories 475; kilojoules 1986; protein 36g; carbohydrate 8g; total fat 32g; saturated fat 8g; monounsaturated fat 14g; cholesterol 144mg; fiber 0g. (**Note:** Figures for fat are approximate since fried foods can absorb as little as 5% of the oil they are cooked in or much, much more. It all depends on the temperature of the oil.)

Old Bay® seasoning is a trademark of Old Bay Company, Inc.
Season-All® seasoned salt is a trademark of Mccormick & Company, Inc.

Chef Series™ Chef's Knife
Chef Series™ 8" Nonstick Fry Pan

Peanut Butter & Company's
Spicy Peanut Butter Burgers

SERVES 8

1½ pounds ground beef or turkey
½ cup The Heat Is On® peanut butter
2 tablespoons unsalted butter
1 yellow onion, grated
1 large egg
3 tablespoons bread crumbs
Olive oil, for the pan

1. Combine the ground meat, peanut butter, butter, onion, egg, and breadcrumbs in a large bowl and knead with your hands until well combined. Make patties about 4 inches wide and ¾ inch thick. Refrigerate for 1 to 2 hours to allow the patties to set and the flavors to meld.

2. Preheat grill.

3. Grill the burgers on an outdoor grill for best results, or fry in a skillet with a small amount of olive oil for 2 to 3 minutes on each side, or until fully cooked inside.

Nutrition per serving: calories 372; kilojoules 1555; protein 26g; carbohydrate 4g; total fat 28g; saturated fat 10g; monounsaturated fat 12g; cholesterol 108mg; fiber 1g.

The Heat Is On™ peanut butter is a trademark of Peanut Butter & Co.

Measuring Spoons
Measuring Cups
Thatsa™ Bowl
Season-Serve® Container

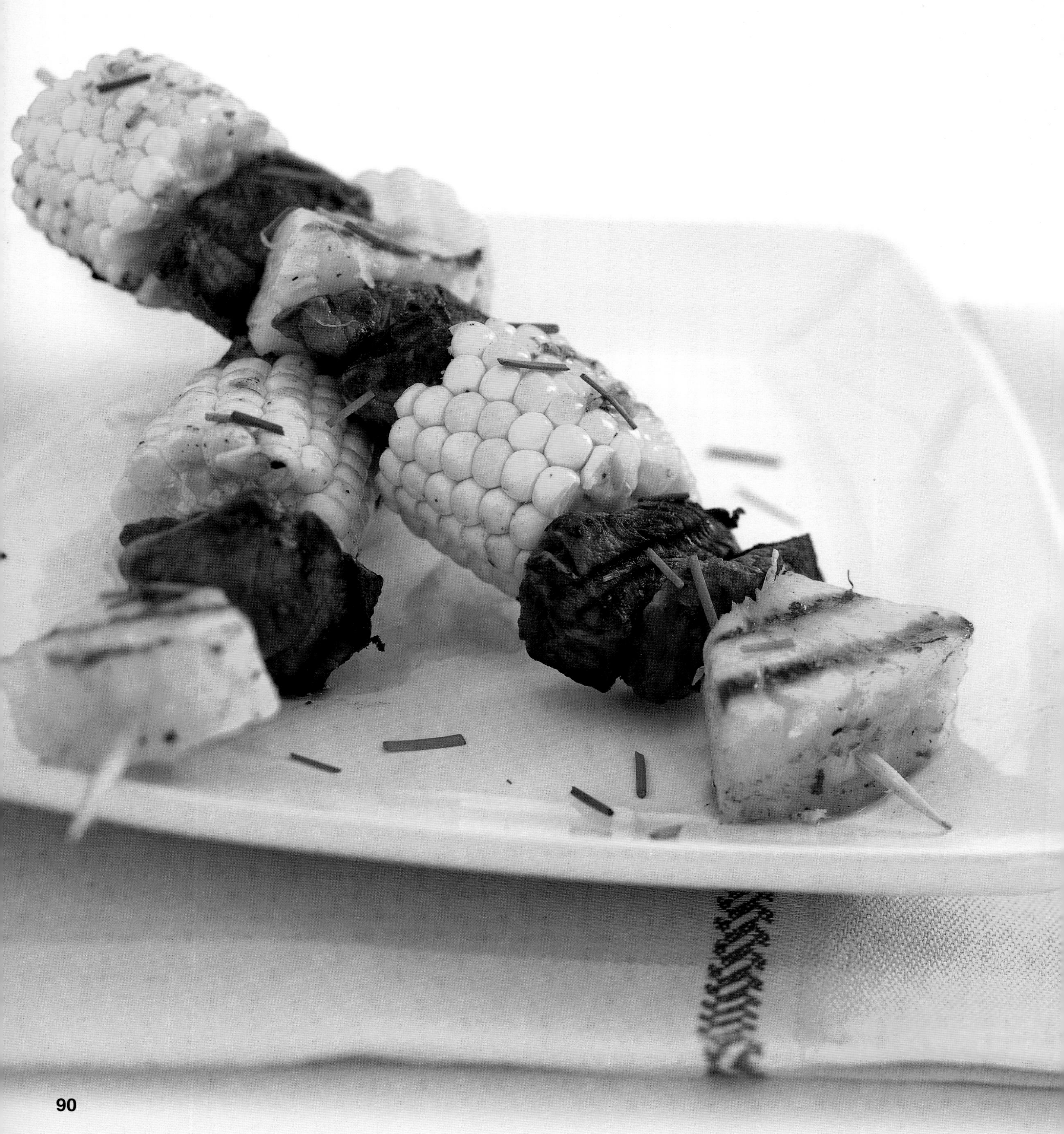

Chevy Chase's Superb Lamb Kabobs

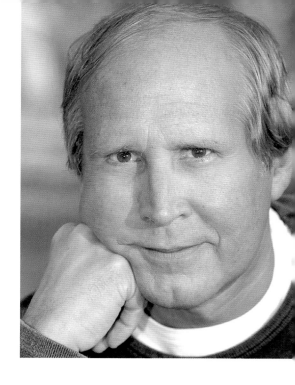

This recipe fascinates me because I love all, and each of the ingredients. I have always, however, loved lamb with either mint sauce or mint jelly. One might try a mint "dip" of some kind with this recipe, despite the pineapple addition. Just the thought of this luscious dish is enough to make my mouth water.

SERVES 12

- **5 lb (1950 g) leg of lamb, boned**
- **2 medium pineapples**
- **1 cup (8 oz/250 ml) red wine**
- **6 tablespoons extra virgin olive oil**
- **4 tablespoons walnut oil**
- **1–2 medium red onions, finely chopped**
- **12 tablespoons fresh basil leaves, chopped**
- **8 cloves of garlic, crushed**
- **Sea salt and fresh black pepper**
- **12 ears of corn**

1. Cube the lamb and pineapples into 1-inch (2.5 cm) pieces. Combine the rest of the ingredients, except for the corn, to make a marinade. Mix the meat with the marinade and refrigerate for 1 day.

2. Prepare and grease grill.

3. Cut the corn into pieces. Slide the corn, pineapple and lamb onto bamboo skewers and grill on high for 10 to 15 minutes. Brush kabobs with the marinade as they cook and turn often. The key here is to monitor the meat with care until it is done the way you like it. Do not let the lamb out of your view, even if it is to frolic with some honey in the pool.

Nutrition per serving: calories 580; kilojoules 2424; protein 33g; carbohydrate 31g; total fat 37g; saturated fat 13g; monounsaturated fat 17g; cholesterol 107mg; fiber 3g.

Quick Chef
Chef Series™ Chef's Knife
Prep Essentials™ Lil' Chopper
Season-Serve® Container
Prep Essentials™ Measuring Cup

Patti D'Arbanville's Peasant Cabbage Fit For A King

Serve this in large bowls with warm crusty French or Italian bread and a nice chilled bottle of sparkling water. Perfect on a chilly evening with a roaring fire.

SERVES 1 (ONLY KIDDING)
SERVES 4–6

Scant ⅛ cup (1 oz /30 g) extra virgin olive oil
8–10 cloves garlic, minced
6 sweet Italian sausages
6 hot Italian sausages
2 large firm heads green cabbage

1. Cover the bottom of a *large* stew pot with the oil and heat gently over a *low* flame. Sauté the garlic — *do not brown*, you just want to sweat it. Squeeze the sausages out of their casings by pinching and squeezing by 1-inch (2.5 cm) increments right into the pot. Brown sausages over a low flame without burning the garlic. When the sausage is golden, slice up the cabbage and put the whole two heads right on top of the sausage. Cover the pan.

2. Stir it all up from the bottom about 10 minutes later and cover again. Keep doing this until the cabbage is cooked down and it all looks and smells delicious. It will be *all* done cooking in an hour or so. The cabbage will have absorbed the sausage flavor by then, but if you can wait to serve it the next day it will be even better. But I bet you won't be able to. I always have to eat it immediately.

Nutrition per serving based on 4 servings: calories 878; kilojoules 3670; protein 49g; carbohydrate 40g; total fat 61g; saturated fat 21g; monounsaturated fat 29g; cholesterol 142mg; fiber 13g.

Easy–Lift™ Cutting Board
Prep Essentials™ Lil' Chopper
Chef Series™ 8 Qt. Stock Pot
Chef Series™ Chef's Knife
Measuring Cups

Marcia Gay Harden's Greens and Couscous

This is a recipe handed down from a dear friend.

SERVES 4

4 cups (1 qt/1 L) of chicken stock
3 andouille sausages, thickly sliced
1 big yellow onion, chopped
1 clove garlic, thinly sliced
2 big bundles (or a big bag) mustard greens and Swiss chard, both or either
2 cups (9 oz/270 g) of cubed yams or sweet potatoes
1 cup (8 fl oz/250 ml) red wine
1 tablespoon chili powder
1 tablespoon thyme
1 tablespoon coriander
1 tablespoon oregano
½ tablespoon of curry or marjoram (optional)
Couscous

1. Bring chicken stock to a boil in a big spaghetti pot. Once stock is boiling add *all* ingredients, except couscous, and stir gently until greens reduce and all ingredients are bathed in the chicken stock. Reduce heat, cover and simmer for 60 minutes or more. (The longer it simmers, the better.) Every 15 minutes or so give it a stir.

2. Make couscous using the pot liquor *instead* of water. Using a perforated soup spoon, spoon greens mixture over couscous in a bowl.

Nutrition with ½ cup couscous per serving: calories 690; kilojoules 2884; protein 29g; carbohydrate 56g; total fat 36g; saturated fat 11g; monounsaturated fat 2g; cholesterol 76mg; fiber 13g.

Chef Series™ 8 Qt. Stock Pot
Quick Chef
Measuring Cups
Measuring Spoons

Isaac Mizrahi's Mac and Cheese

Who doesn't love macaroni and cheese? It's the white-trashiest I get while remaining Jewish. This recipe was commandeered from Ilene Weinberg.

SERVES 6

1 lb/500 g macaroni
¼ cup (2 oz/60 g) butter
¼ cup (1.25 oz/35 g) all-purpose (plain) flour
1 cup (8 fl oz/250 ml) milk
1 cup (8 fl oz/250 ml) cream
4 cups (1 lb/500 g) cheddar cheese, grated
4 cups (1 lb/500 g) Muenster cheese, grated
Some salt
Some freshly ground pepper
Some freshly grated nutmeg

1. Preheat oven to 350°F (180°C).

2. Bring water (enough to cook the pasta — about 4 quarts) to a boil.

3. To make the béchamel sauce, heat the milk and cream together in a small saucepan, making sure it doesn't boil.

4. In a heavy bottom saucepan, over low heat, melt the butter and whisk in the flour briskly until the mixture is smoothly blended. (Do not allow it to change color.) Gradually add the hot milk and cream mixture and bring it all to a boil, whisking well to prevent any lumps. Season with salt and pepper and a grating or two or four of nutmeg. Simmer the sauce gently for 3–5 minutes, stirring a little here and there.

5. Meanwhile, cook the macaroni for about 8 minutes.

6. Once the white sauce is made, combine it with the macaroni and put it in a baking pan that has been buttered. Cover with all that cheese. No kidding, it's so good.

7. Bake it for half an hour, or a little longer if you want it crispier. (If you have a convection feature on your oven, congratulations. It'll be golden brown either way.)

Nutrition per serving based on 6 servings: calories 868; kilojoules 3628; protein 39g; carbohydrate 49g; total fat 57g; saturated fat 36g; monounsaturated fat 16g; cholesterol 182mg; fiber 2g.

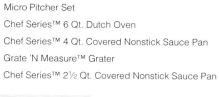

Micro Pitcher Set
Chef Series™ 6 Qt. Dutch Oven
Chef Series™ 4 Qt. Covered Nonstick Sauce Pan
Grate 'N Measure™ Grater
Chef Series™ 2½ Qt. Covered Nonstick Sauce Pan

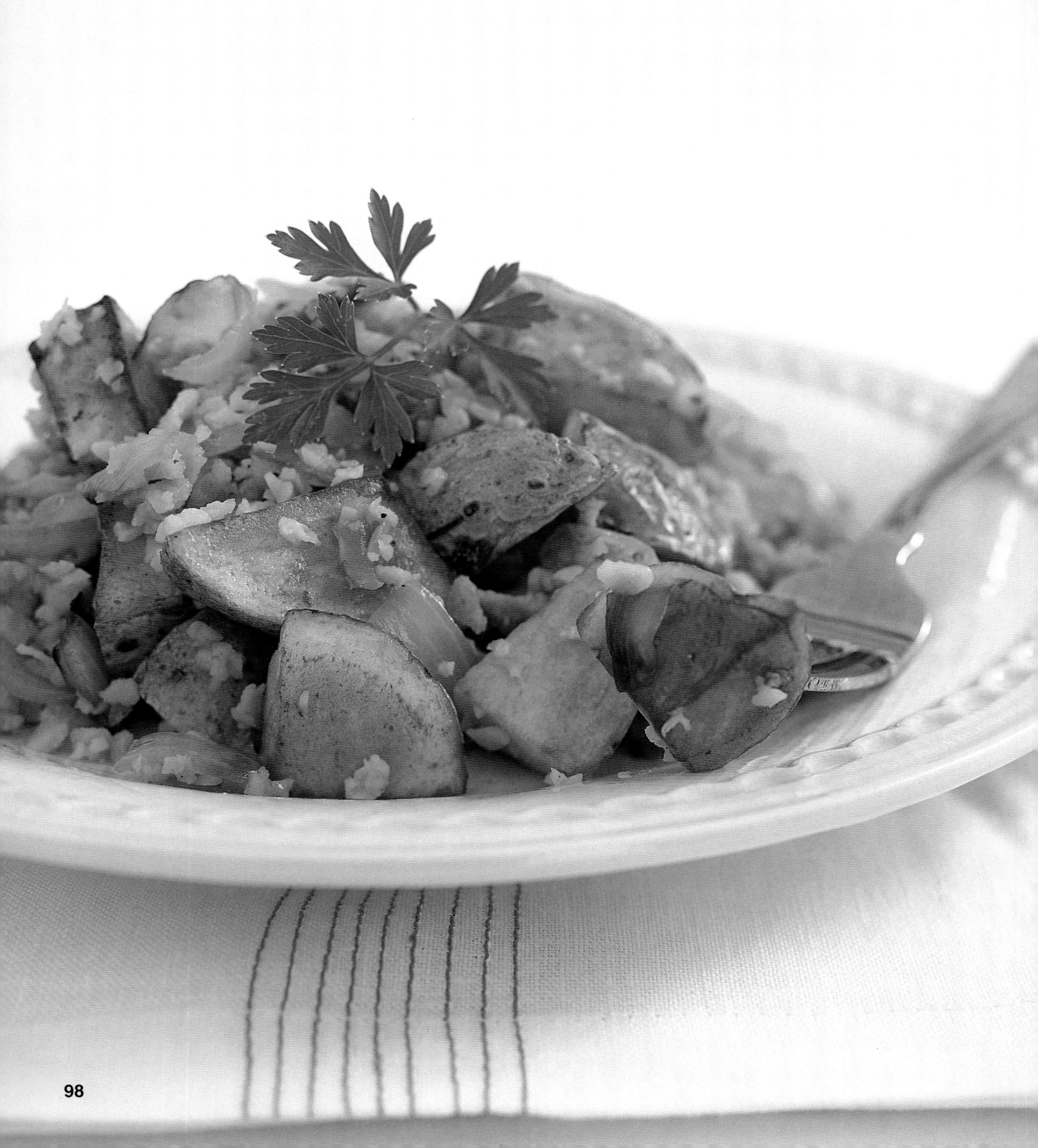

Alan Cumming's Stovies

Stovies is a Scottish dish that is traditionally made with lard and minced beef, but I am a vegetarian so I have made up my own version. It is real peasant food and ideal for people who, like me, like to have a plateful of one thing. I much prefer a mush-style dish to something with loads of different components.

SERVES 8

Olive oil
3–4 cloves garlic
4 biggish onions
8–10 biggish potatoes
Tamari (dark soybean sauce)
Worcestershire sauce
Salt and pepper to taste
Textured vegetable protein (TVP)

1. Put a good sloosh of olive oil into a wok or large pot. I normally turn the bottle upside down and count to four.

2. Chop 4 cloves, more if you like, and fry them in the olive oil. Allow the oil to permeate the garlic but don't let them to get crispy. They will make a tasty base for the stovies.

3. Cut up the 4 onions and into fairly big chunks and add them to the olive oil and garlic. Fry them for a bit longer; then put a lid on the pot and leave them to sweat for five minutes.

4. Scrub and cut up enough potatoes to at least double the quantity of the onions. Chop them into fairly big mouthful size chunks. Add the potatoes to the sweating onions and garlic and leave them for a bit to get all infused.

5. Now comes the fun bit. Add about 20 squirts of Tamari into the wok, then do the same with your Worcestershire sauce. You could also use barbecue sauce or something similar. Basically, the trick is to make the stovies tasty and to give them a bit of a brown color. You do all this to your taste. You can also add some salt and pepper if you like (although don't go crazy with the salt if you are going heavy on the tamari).

6. Then throw in a couple of big handfuls of the TVP, aka textured vegetable protein. It swells up in the water and gives the stovies nice texture and taste and also makes them thicker. So if your stovies are too runny throw some more in to thicken it up.

7. Pour water into the wok so that all the ingredients are just submerged. Bring to a boil for a few minutes and reduce to simmer for 30 minutes with the lid half on, half off. Stir occasionally. Once the potatoes are cooked, give them a little beating up with a spoon to make the stovies mushier. Then you can turn them off, put the lid on, and let them cook in their own juices.

8. I don't really do precise measurements when I cook. Basically this is a mushy potato stewy thing that can come in various consistencies. You just have to find the combination that suits you best. You can also add things like hot sauce or mustard if you feel daring. Stovies are so great for parties on cold winter nights because you can just leave them on the stove and people can help themselves throughout the night as they please. Enjoy!

Nutrition per serving: calories 495; kilojoules 2069; protein 33g; carbohydrate 82g; total fat 8g; saturated fat 1g; monounsaturated fat 5g; cholesterol 0mg; fiber 14g.

Chef Series™ Chef's Knife
Chef Series™ 9½" Covered Nonstick Fry Pan
Prep Essentials™ Lil' Chopper
Saucy Silicone Spatula

Debra Messing's Radiatore Pasta Sauce

SERVES 4–6

2 tablespoons olive oil
½ cup (2–3 oz/60–90 g) carrots
½ cup (2–3 oz/60–90 g) onions
2 garlic cloves
¼ (1 oz/30 g) raisins
½ cup (2–3 oz/60–90 g) red bell pepper
2 (28 oz/850 g) cans crushed tomatoes
Red wine
Sugar (optional)
Crushed red pepper flakes
Salt and pepper
1 lb (500 g) cooked radiatore pasta
4 oz (125 g) feta cheese

1. Sauté carrots, onions, garlic, raisins, and red bell peppers in olive oil. (You can also add tomato paste and/or pork sausage.) Remove from heat and set aside.

2. Take large cans of crushed tomatoes — a minimum of two (you can use more for more sauce) — and place in saucepan. Add red wine and sautéed ingredients, and simmer until sauce is the consistency you prefer. (You can add sugar if it is too acidic.)

3. While simmering sauce, add spicy red pepper flakes, salt, and pepper to taste.

4. Put sauce in a serving dish with cooked radiatore pasta; mix together while hot, and then crumble drained feta cheese on top. Serve with extra feta.

Nutrition per serving based on 4 servings: calories 727; kilojoules 3039; protein 27g; carbohydrate 124g; total fat 15g; saturated fat 6g; monounsaturated fat 6g; cholesterol 25mg; fiber 12g.

Chef Series™ Chef's Knife
Chef Series™ 4 Qt. Covered Nonstick Sauce Pan
Easy-Lift™ Cutting Board
Saucy Silicone Spatula

Lisa Rinna's Bolognese Sauce

SERVES 6–8

½ white onion

5 cloves garlic

1 lb (500 g) ground sirloin

1 tablespoon soy sauce

Salt

2 cans (28 oz/840 g) whole tomatoes

2 (6 oz/180 g) cans tomato paste

1 tablespoon olive oil

3 sprigs fresh rosemary

1 tablespoon balsamic vinegar

1 cup cabernet (red wine)

3 tablespoons honey

1. Slice onion into small pieces and place into a large frying pan. Add two cloves of garlic cut cross the grain into thin slices (about 5 slices per clove). Add the ground sirloin and spread into the pan. Sprinkle soy sauce over the meat and cook over a low flame until just brown throughout. Add salt to taste.

2. Slice remaining garlic and add to a large saucepan with tomatoes, tomato paste, olive oil, two sprigs of rosemary, vinegar, and cabernet.

3. Strip the leaves from the remaining sprig of rosemary and chop into small pieces. Add half of the chopped rosemary to the saucepan. Stir and bring contents to a boil. Reduce heat and simmer until the tomatoes have disintegrated, about 10 to 15 minutes. (Use a wooden spoon to help break up the tomatoes.) Add the ground sirloin mixture. Stir in honey to taste, approximately three tablespoons. Simmer for 45 minutes, adding more wine to taste.

Nutrition per serving of sauce only: calories 272; kilojoules 1137; protein 20g; carbohydrate 33g; total fat 6g; saturated fat 2g; monounsaturated fat 3g; cholesterol 40mg; fiber 6g.

Easy-Lift™ Cutting Board
Chef Series™ 8 Qt. Stock Pot
Chef Series™ Chef's Knife
Measuring Spoons

Sweet Endings

Patricia Clarkson's Praline Parfait

SERVES 10

1½ cups (1 lb/500 g) light Karo® corn syrup
½ cup (4 oz/120 g) brown sugar
3 tablespoons butter
¼ teaspoon salt
2 tablespoons all-purpose (plain) flour
½ cup (4 fl oz/125 ml) water
2 teaspoons vanilla extract
½ cup (2 oz/60 g) chopped pecans
20 scoops of vanilla ice cream

1. Dissolve and combine Karo® syrup, brown sugar, butter, and salt and cook over low heat (until sugar is dissolved). Stir in flour, one tablespoon at a time. Add water and mix well. Bring to boil; boil for 10 minutes. Remove from heat and let cool for 1 to 2 hours. Add vanilla and pecans. Mix well.

2. Drizzle praline mixture over two scoops of vanilla ice cream. Serve and enjoy!

Nutrition per serving: calories 520; kilojoules 2174; protein 5g; carbohydrate 80g; total fat 22g; saturated fat 11g; monounsaturated fat 7g; cholesterol 67mg; fiber 2g. **Note:** Nutrition analysis is based on each scoop of ice cream measuring about ½ cup (2 ½ oz /75 g).

Karo® corn syrup is a trademark of Ach Food Companies, Inc.

Chef Series™ 8" Nonstick Fry Pan
Quick Chef
Measuring Cups
Measuring Spoons
Micro Pitcher Set
Saucy Silicone Spatula

Marilu Henner's Chocolate Almond Toffee Crunch

SERVES 24

1 sleeve all natural crackers (such as Health Valley low-fat whole wheat crackers)
1 cup (8 oz/250 g) Earth Balance® buttery spread
½ cup Sucanat® sweetener
3 ounces sliced almonds
12 ounces semisweet chocolate chips (Sunspire® grain sweetened or any other non-dairy chocolate chips)

1. Preheat oven to 375°F (190°C).

2. Line a cookie sheet with foil, making sure it goes up the sides. Place a single layer of crackers on the sheet, covering it.

3. Melt the buttery spread and the Sucanat® in a small saucepan, whisking the whole time just until it starts to froth and turn golden brown. (Do not let the Sucanat® caramelize.) Pour the mixture over the crackers, using a spatula to cover the crackers as evenly as you can. Bake immediately for 7 minutes, or until caramel colored. Sprinkle the crackers with almonds and then the chocolate chips and bake for 2 to 3 minutes more, or until the chips are soft. Swirl the chips with a butter knife to spread the chocolate over the surface. Cool, and then refrigerate about 30 minutes until the chocolate is set. Cut or break into pieces. Store in the refrigerator.

Nutrition per serving: calories 185; kilojoules 773; protein 2g; carbohydrate 16g; total fat 13g; saturated fat 5g; monounsaturated fat 3g; cholesterol 0mg; fiber 2g.

Earth Balance® buttery spread is a trademark of GFA Brands, Inc.
Sucanat® sweetener is a trademark of Ragus Holdings, Inc.
Sunspire® grain is a trademark of nSpired Natural Foods Corporation

Recipe courtesy Marilu Henner, *Party Hearty: Hot, Sexy, Have-a-Blast Food & Fun All Year Round*, previously published as *Healthy Holidays*, HarperCollins Publishers, 2003.

Saucy Silicone Spatula
Measuring Cups
Chef Series™ Jelly Roll Pan

Chef Gontran Cherrier's Strawberry and Raspberry Salad With Granita of Schweppes®

I chose this recipe as it can be made in two different versions: light or classical. In fact, I make it a point of honour to create pastry recipes which contain very little sugar and are low fat, as often as possible, and also according to individual tastes. I generally like the bitter taste in a dessert when it is balanced with the fruit taste, as it is with this recipe. Concerning the low calorie possibility, I suggest using classic or light Schweppes® tonic water, as you like. Enjoy the Granita.

It is important to use red fruits of very tasty, very good quality in order to emphasize the contrast between the bitterness of the granite (a slushy, flavoured ice) and the sweet taste of the red fruits. You can make this dessert with light or classic tonic water. The light version is perfect for people who like bitter flavour, and if the fruits are in season. Concerning strawberries, I would advise using Maras des Bois or Gariguettes.

SERVES 6–8

- 1⅓ cups (700 ml) of Schweppes® tonic water
- 15 oz (450 g) raspberries
- 1 lb (500 g) strawberries
- 1 large spoon of powdered (icing) sugar
- Zest of 1 lemon
- Juice of 1 lemon

1. Start the preparation of the granita at least 4 hours before the meal. To make it, pour the Schweppes into a shallow dish and place in freezer and stir with a fork every 30 minutes or until it is icy, as the aim is to obtain flakes. If the granita is not mixed regularly, it becomes a solid block of ice.

2. Finish the preparation of the granita about 1 hour before serving. Remove it from the dish by putting lukewarm water on the bottom of the dish, without letting it melt. Break it into large pieces. Put it in a bowl of a mixer and reduce it into tiny pieces. Keep in the refrigerator.

3. Repeat this operation just before serving the dessert, using a fork: the more the granita will be mixed, the finer will be the powder. The granita must be very fine, like snow.

4. To prepare the strawberries, cut them into slices, not too thin. Put them in a small bowl and pour on the sugar, the lemon juice, and lemon zest. Mix and keep in the refrigerator.

5. To serve, put a large spoon of granita in the bottom of each serving glass. Add about 15 raspberries, then 3 large spoons of granita, and 2 large spoons of strawberries without too much juice. To finish, add 2 or 3 large spoons of granite on top. (This is a dessert which must be served immediately, because once the granita has melted, the charm disappears.)

   Additional trick: You can put the Schweppes® tonic water into the freezer the night before and reduce it into powder the evening of the dinner. You can serve the dessert in a large and low glass and make a cocktail presentation. To do that, cut a lime into slices and put it on the rim of the glass. Squeeze lime juice into the preparation, if you like.

Nutrition per serving: calories 77; kilojoules 322; protein 1g; carbohydrate 23g; total fat 0g; saturated fat 0g; monounsaturated fat 0g; cholesterol 0mg; fiber 7g.

Schweppes® tonic water is a trademark of Schweppes International Limited

Prep Essentials™ Citrus Wonder™ Juicer
Prep Essentials™ Measuring Cup
Easy–Lift™ Cutting Board
Chef Series™ 4" Utility Knife
Prep Essentials™ Large Mixing Bowl Set

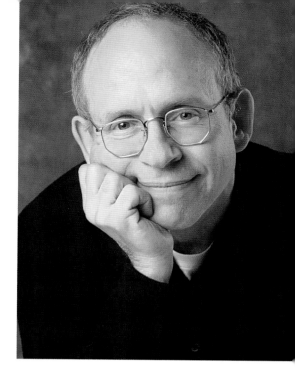

Bob Balaban's Mocha Cheesecake

This is the cake my wife, Lynn Grossman, is asked to bake for birthdays, Thanksgiving, and all special occasions. It's easy to make, and — not to be immodest about this — completely delicious. It will feed 12 people in New York or 18 people in LA, maybe more.

SERVES 12

CRUST:

¾ cup (2 oz/60 g) graham cracker (wafer) crumbs

¼ cup (2 oz/60 g) unsalted butter, melted

6 tablespoons sugar

FILLING:

24 oz/750 g cream cheese, softened and cut into cubes for easy beating

2 eggs

1 cup (7 oz/200 g) sugar

8 oz/250 g semi-sweet chocolate, melted

2 tablespoons heavy cream

7 tablespoons strong coffee or espresso

½ cup (4 oz/120 g) sour cream

1. Preheat the oven to 350°F (180°C).

2. You can buy graham cracker crumbs, or make your own in a food processor. Or try putting graham crackers in a plastic bag and hitting the bag and rolling over it with a rolling pin until the crackers are crumby. It's a lot of fun. If you want, instead of using graham crackers you can use chocolate wafers, vanilla wafers, shortbread, chocolate grahams, cinnamon grahams, etc., for the crust.

3. To make the crust, mix all ingredients together. You can do this by hand. Press whatever mixture you have into the bottom of an 8-inch (20 cm) springform pan until it covers the bottom. Set the pan aside and prepare the filling.

4. Put cream cheese, eggs and sugar into a food processor and process or mix until smooth. Alternately, mix with a hand mixer. Add remaining ingredients and process, or beat, until really, really, really, smooth. Pour cream cheese mixture into prepared pan. Bake for 1 hour. (Unless you have a springform pan with a lip to catch drips, put your pan on a baking sheet to catch the drips). When done, the cake should be slightly wiggly in the middle. It will firm up as it cools. If the middle looks really soft and mushy, cook it longer. About 15–20 minutes ought to do it. Cool the cake on a rack and then refrigerate.

5. Take cake out of the refrigerator a half-hour before serving. Run a knife carefully around the inside of the pan and open the springform. Use a spatula to carefully get the pan bottom off the cake.

Nutrition per serving: calories 474; kilojoules 1981; protein 7g; carbohydrate 41g; total fat 34g; saturated fat 20g; monounsaturated fat 10g; cholesterol 115mg; fiber 11g.

Measuring Spoons

Measuring Cups

Micro Pitcher Set

Wonderlier® Bowl Set

Chef Series™ 4" Utility Knife

Kitchen Duos

Barbara Mandrell's Aspen Snowballs

This is one of my family's favorite Aspen recipes. It originated at a restaurant Ken and I visited in Aspen some twenty-five years ago. It's such a pain to prepare… just imagine making a snowball out of ice cream without wearing gloves! You really do have to love someone to want to make it for them. When Mathew was in high school, I made these for him and the whole football team. Everyone raved about them so my cold hands were worth it. NO PAIN, NO GAIN!

SERVES 1

Shredded sweetened coconut
Vanilla ice cream
Hot fudge sauce

1. Preheat oven to 300°F (170°C).

2. Brown the coconut lightly on a cookie sheet in a 300°F (170°C) oven. Let cool.

3. Mold the ice cream, using your hands, into a snowball-size ball. (Have lukewarm water running; your hands will get cold.) Roll the ice cream ball in toasted coconut and place it in the freezer. Heat the hot fudge in a stovetop double boiler or in a microwave oven. Spoon hot fudge onto a small plate and place the snowball in the center.

Nutrition per serving: calories 324; kilojoules 1354; protein 4g; carbohydrate 45g; total fat 15g; saturated fat 10g; monounsaturated fat 4g; cholesterol 30mg; fiber 2g. **Note:** The nutrition analysis includes ½ cup (2½ oz/75 g) ice cream and 2 tablespoons of both the coconut and hot fudge sauce.

Chef Series™ Jelly Roll Pan
Silicone Wonder™ Mat
Ice Cream Scoop
Heat 'N Serve™ Oval Containers

Mike Myers' Nanaimo Bars

SERVES 16

BASE (CRUST):

- ½ cup (4 oz/120 g) butter
- ¼ cup (2 oz/60 g) sugar
- 5 tablespoons cocoa
- 1 egg, slightly beaten
- 1 teaspoon vanilla extract (essence)
- 2 cups (6 oz/180 g) graham cracker (wafer) crumbs
- 1 cup (2½ oz) shredded sweetened coconut
- ½ cup (2 oz/60 g) chopped walnuts

VANILLA FILLING:

- ¼ cup (1 oz/30 g) butter
- ¼ cup (2 fl oz/125 ml) milk
- 2 tablespoons custard powder
- 2 cups (9 oz/270 g) confectioners' (icing) sugar
- 1 teaspoon vanilla extract (essence)

TOPPING:

- 4 (1 oz/30 g) squares semi-sweet chocolate
- 1 tablespoon butter

1. To make the base (crust), combine butter, sugar, cocoa, and egg in a saucepan over low heat. Cook and stir until thick and smooth, about 5 minutes. Remove from heat and stir in vanilla extract (essence.) Add graham cracker (wafer) crumbs, coconut, and nuts. Stir to mix. Spread in a greased 9-inch (22.5 cm) square pan and pack down firmly.

2. To make vanilla filling, cream the butter. Combine milk and custard powder and blend until smooth. Stir custard mixture into the butter. Add confectioners' (icing) sugar and blend on low speed with mixer until smooth. Stir in vanilla extract (essence). Spread filling over base layer. Chill for 15 minutes.

3. To make the topping, melt chocolate and butter together. Spread over the filling. Refrigerate until firm. Cut into bars and serve.

   Note: If you can't find custard powder, 2–3 tablespoons of instant vanilla pudding makes a fine substitute, although the flavor will be slightly different.

Nutrition per serving: calories 293; kilojoules 1225; protein 3g; carbohydrate 35g; total fat 17g; saturated fat 9g; monounsaturated fat 4g; cholesterol 38mg; fiber 2g.

Chef Series™ 2½ Qt. Covered Nonstick Sauce Pan

Quick Chef

Measuring Spoons

Measuring Cups

Saucy Silicone Spatula

Micro Pitcher Set

Patti LaBelle's Peach Upside-Down Cake

I picked this recipe because it really reminds me of my mother. She made the best peach upside-down cake in the world and every time I make it, it brings back all those great memories of cooking with her and learning from her. It just reminds me of my childhood and being around all of my family!

I like to use an 8-inch (20 cm) cast iron skillet when I make this cake. If you can't find fresh peaches, you can use two 15-ounce cans of sliced light freestone peaches in extra light syrup, drained.

SERVES 10

2 tablespoons packed light brown sugar
2 tablespoons brown sugar substitute
¾ cup (⅔ oz/18 g) sugar substitute, divided
2 tablespoons plus ⅓ cup (2½ oz/75 g) margarine
2 ripe peaches, peeled, pitted and sliced (about 2 cups)
½ teaspoon grated nutmeg
1½ cups (6 oz/180 g) cake (soft-wheat) flour
½ teaspoon baking powder
¼ teaspoon salt
3 tablespoons sugar
1 egg
1 teaspoon vanilla extract (essence)
1 teaspoon butter flavor extract (essence)
½ cup (4 fl oz/125 ml) fat-free half and half

1. Preheat oven to 350°F (180°C).

2. In a small bowl, stir together the brown sugar, brown sugar substitute, and ¼ cup of the sugar substitute.

3. In an 8-inch or 10-inch ovenproof skillet, melt 2 tablespoons of the margarine. Sprinkle evenly with the sugar mixture. Arrange the peach slices in the pan in overlapping concentric circles starting from the center. Sprinkle with nutmeg.

4. In a medium bowl, combine the flour, baking powder and salt.

5. In a large bowl, beat the remaining ⅓ cup margarine until light, about 30 seconds. Beat in the sugar and remaining ½ cup sugar substitute until light and fluffy, about 30 seconds.

6. Beat in the egg, vanilla extract (essence), and butter flavor extract (extract).

7. Beat in the flour mixture alternately with the half and half, beating for 30 seconds. Spoon the batter over the peaches.

8. Bake until lightly golden and a toothpick inserted in the center of the cake comes out clean, 30 to 35 minutes. Invert onto a serving plate and replace any topping that might have fallen off.

Nutrition per serving: calories 196; kilojoules 819; protein 3g; carbohydrate 27g; total fat 9g; saturated fat 2g; monounsaturated fat 4g; cholesterol 21mg; fiber 1g.

Prep Essentials™ Mini Mixing Bowl Set
Prep Essentials™ Large Mixing Bowl Set
Chef Series™ 8" Nonstick Fry Pan
Measuring Cups
Saucy Silicone Spatula

Molly Ringwald's Mom Mom's Poppyseed Cake

SERVES 16

CAKE:

1¼ (6 oz/180 g) cups poppy seeds

1 cup (8 fl oz/250 ml) buttermilk

1 cup (8 oz/250 g) unsalted butter

1½ cups (10 oz/300 g) sugar

4 eggs

2½ cups (12½ oz/375 g) all-purpose (plain) flour

2 teaspoons baking powder

1 teaspoon baking soda

½ teaspoon salt

1 teaspoon vanilla extract (essence)

SUGAR MIXTURE:

¼ cup (2 oz/60 g) sugar

1 teaspoon cinnamon

GLAZE:

1 cup (4½ oz/135 g) sifted confectioners' (icing) sugar

1 tablespoon butter, softened

2 tablespoons milk

¼ teaspoon vanilla extract (essence)

A pinch of salt

1. To make cake, soak poppy seeds in buttermilk overnight.

2. Preheat oven to 350°F (180°C.)

3. Cream butter and sugar well. Add eggs, one at a time. Beat until light and fluffy.

4. Sift flour, baking powder, baking soda and salt together three times. Stir flour mixture into butter-sugar mixture, alternately with the buttermilk mixture. Add vanilla extract (essence). Spoon half of batter into a well-greased bundt or Kuglehoff pan. Sprinkle with two-thirds of the sugar mixture. Top with remaining batter and sprinkle with the remaining sugar mixture.

5. Bake at 350°F (180°C) for approximately one hour. Cool cake in pan for 10 minutes; turn out on a rack and glaze.

6. To make the glaze, beat butter into confectioners' sugar. Add milk and beat until glaze is proper consistency. Add vanilla extract (essence) and salt. Pour glaze over cake. Glaze will drip down sides of warm cake, giving it a rustic appearance. (If glaze drips all the way off, scoop it back onto the cake.)

Nutrition per serving: calories 377; kilojoules 1576; protein 6g; carbohydrate 48g; total fat 19g; saturated fat 9g; monounsaturated fat 4g; cholesterol 86mg; fiber 2g.

Measuring Cups

Measuring Spoons

Thatsa™ Bowl

Prep Essentials™ Measuring Cup

Saucy Silicone Spatula

Chef Series™ Seasoning Blend

Glossary & Index

Glossary

Chef Series™ 9½" Covered Nonstick Fry Pan
Perfect for searing meat, this fry pan features Tri-Ply construction with a core layer of aluminum sandwiched between two layers of heavy, 18-gauge stainless steel. Amongst the highest quality cookware on the market. This Pan also features nonstick coating and is safe to use on all cooking surfaces, including gas, electric, ceramic and induction. Tempered glass cover is oven safe to 350°F.

Chef Series™ 2½ Quart Covered Nonstick Sauce Pan
Functional size with nonstick coating and dual pouring lips. Quality Tri-Ply construction is safe to use on all cooking surfaces, including gas, electric, ceramic and induction. Tempered glass cover is oven safe to 350°F.

Chef Series™ 3 Quart Casserole
This casserole features durable 18-gauge stainless steel-for a lifetime of enjoyment. Quality Tri-Ply construction is safe to use on all cooking surfaces, including gas, electric, ceramic and induction. Encapsulated bases produce fast and even heating. This casserole features a nonstick cooking surface.

Chef Series™ 4 Quart Covered Nonstick Sauce Pan
This Sauce Pan is perfect for risottos, smaller quantities of soups and casseroles. The Pan features two pouring lips and nonstick coating with Tri-Ply construction is safe to use on all cooking surfaces including gas, electric, ceramic, induction and in the oven. Tempered glass cover is oven safe to 350°F.

Chef Series™ 6 Quart Dutch Oven
This Dutch oven is great when entertaining a large crowd. Features a stainless steel cover and Tri-Ply construction, which makes it safe to use on all cooking surfaces including gas, electric, ceramic, induction and in the oven.

Chef Series™ 6 Quart Nonstick Covered Sauté Pan
Wide, flat bottom with high sides perfect for frying chicken or sautéing vegetables. Featuring Tri-Ply construction, this Pan is safe to use on all cooking surfaces, including gas, electric, ceramic, induction and in the oven. Tempered glass cover is oven safe to 350°F.

Chef Series™ 8 Quart Stock Pot
Large capacity is a must have for soups and pasta. Capacity markings inside Pot make it easy to see how much you have on hand. Features Tri-Ply construction, making it safe to use on all cooking surfaces including gas, electric, ceramic, induction and in the oven. Tempered glass cover is oven safe to 350°F.

Chef Series™ 8" Nonstick Fry Pan
Perfect for preparing omelet's or dinner side dishes, this Fry Pan features the same Tri-Ply construction and high quality nonstick coating as the

9½" Fry Pan. Safe to use on all cooking surfaces, including gas, electric, ceramic, induction and in the oven.

Chef Series™ 3½" Paring Knife
Part of the professional-grade Chef Series™ Knives, this versatile knife performs a wide range of everyday cutting. Forged from the finest Japanese stainless steel, this Paring Knife is shaped to offer optimum comfort and performance for any task.

Chef Series™ 4" Utility Knife
Part of the professional-grade Chef Series™ Knives, this knife is ideal for work requiring control and precision like peeling, scraping or pitting.

Chef Series™ Chef's Knife
From the contoured and perfectly balanced handles to the exceptional cutting edge of the forged, hand-polished stainless steel blades, experience uncompromising performance from our professional-grade knives. Part of the professional-grade Chef Series™ Knives, this knife easily cuts through chops, steaks and other raw or cooked meats as well as large vegetables and fresh herbs.

Chef Series™ Jelly Roll Pan
This Pan features a heavy-gauge, aluminized stainless-steel construction with a DuPont® TEFLON® nonstick coating. 38 x 25 cm / 15" x 10".

Chef Series™ Oval Roaster
A must for preparing traditional family recipes, this Roaster features stainless steel Tri-Ply construction with a nonstick rack. 16"L x 11"W x 4"H.

Chef Series™ Seasoning Blends
Spice blends to give foods a unique taste. Add a few simple ingredients to make delicious marinades, dips, mixes and salad dressings.

Clear Impressions™ Large Bowl
Great for storing and serving large main dishes. Make food ahead of time, store in fridge and then take along to casual get-togethers. 18-cup capacity.

Easy-Lift™ Cutting Board
Make easy work of any cutting job with this cleverly designed cutting board. Four non-skid feet enable you to chop safely and effortlessly, while two cutaway handles allow easy pickup.

E-Series™ Can Opener
Ergonomic handle and turning gear makes opening cans with minimal sharp edges a breeze. Patented gripper lifts lid right off the can.

Grate 'N Measure™ Grater
Supported by a container with a handle, this grater stands at an angle for

a natural grating motion. Perfect for grating soft cheeses, chocolate and vegetables. 2½-cup sheer measuring bin with stainless steel blade.

Heat 'N Serve™ Oval Containers
Store, freeze, reheat and serve, all in one container. Raised hub in center of base ensures even heating of contents, from center to edge. 3-cup (700 mL) Round Container, 4¾-cup (1.1 L) Oval Container, 6¼-cup (1.5 L) Round Container, and 8¼-cup (2 L) Oval Container.

Ice Cream Scoop
Soft-grip ergonomic handle on this professional-style scoop — even hard frozen ice cream is no match for this scoop. Sharply tapered scoop glides easily through any frozen confection.

Kitchen Duos
Multi-function tools snap together for a variety of serving pieces. Heat resistant up to 425°F and safe for use with nonstick cooking surfaces.

Measuring Cups
More sizes than most, and they nest for storage. Featuring six Measuring Cups with pour spouts on both sides: ¼, ⅓, ½, ⅔, ¾, and 1-cup capacities.

Measuring Spoons
Tupperware's combination of smart features and contemporary design make this set a modern day classic. Six Spoons with detachable ring sit level on the counter: ⅛, ¼, ½ and 1 tsp; plus ½ and 1 Tbsp. capacities.

Micro Pitcher Set
Microwave-safe pitchers for melting butter, chocolate, glazes and more. Standard and metric measurements. 1 and 2-cup pitchers.

Prep Essentials™ Citrus Wonder™ Juicer
Unique shape includes a smaller point for lemons, limes and smaller oranges; widened base is for larger oranges and grapefruit. Base features both small and large holes, which allow you to regulate the amount of pulp in the juice. It even zests!

Prep Essentials™ Large Mixing Bowl Set
Sturdy, lightweight Mixing Bowl features a splatter guard, seal, secure-grip handle and wide, non-drip pouring spout. Perfect for preparing, storing and transporting batter and dough. 3-qt. capacity.

Prep Essentials™ Lil' Chopper
Chop everything from onions to ham with just a twist of your hands. The faster you turn it, the more finely it chops. Non-slip base also provides for secure, one-handed use on countertop.

Prep Essentials™ Measuring Cup
Designed for handy liquid measurements. Standard and metric measure-

ments on the inside and outside of the cup for easy viewing. Angled measuring lines help track quantity poured. 2-cup capacity.

Prep Essentials™ Mini Mixing Bowl
Ideal for preparing dips, salsa and sauces, or staging ingredients for recipes. 2-cup capacity with seal.

Prep Essentials™ Mix-N-Stor® Plus Pitcher
Measure, mix, pour and store, all from one pitcher. Features a removable Splatter Guard to eliminate making a countertop mess while mixing, while center seal allows for easy storage of leftovers. 2-qt. capacity.

Quick Chef
A few quick turns are all it takes to chop, mix and whisk fruits, vegetables and more. Non-skid base prevents sliding. Includes chopping blade, paddle whisk and funnel attachments. Standard and metric measurements.

Saucy Silicone Spatula
Ideal for combining batters, cake mixes and stirring on the stovetop. Heat-resistant up to 400°F. Stain-resistant.

Season-Serve® Container
No more messy marinades! The smartest marinator in the world; built-in grids enable marinade to flow around food for superior coverage and flavor. Also ideal for breading, flouring and defrosting.

Silicone Wonder™ Mat
Flexible silicone liner for cookie sheets and baking pans. Safe for use in freezer, microwave and conventional ovens up to 425°F. Cleans quickly with hot, soapy water.

Thatsa® Bowl
Multipurpose Bowl with built-in thumb handle gives you a superior grip and reduces fatigue when preparing a variety of foods and recipes from cookie dough to garden-fresh salads. 32-cup capacity.

Vertical Peeler
For right or left hand. Dishwasher safe, this peeler features a stainless steel blade that makes thin strips effortlessly.

Wonderlier® Bowl Set
Set of all-purpose bowls great for preparing, storing and serving. Set of 3 features 6-cup (1.4 L), 8¾-cup (2.1 L) and 12-cup (2.8 L) capacity bowls.

Index

Acknowledgments

Tupperware® Cooks! is not the work of any one person, but the product of many people who saw the potential of bringing the iconic Tupperware® brand together with New York City's Drama Dept. to create this incredible collection of delectable recipes and innovative products. The result is this stunning cookbook!

Tupperware Brands Corporation would like to express their gratitude to all those who have participated in the production of this book.

SPECIAL THANKS GO TO:
The gracious Celebrities and Chefs who donated their favorite recipes.
The Tupperware® teams in Austria, France, Germany, Japan, Mexico, Spain, and Orlando, Florida, for their time and efforts in translating and producing *Tupperware® Cooks!*
Drama Dept. executives Michael S. Rosenberg, Douglas Carter Beane, and especially Alana O'Brien, for her tireless assistance with all aspects of the cookbook collaboration.
Friends of Drama Dept.: Heather Hurley, Myra Scheer, and Abe Gurko.
Drama Dept. Board of Directors: Steve Bozemen, Robin Brown, Gil Garfield, Stuart Gelwarg, Kitty Carlisle Hart, Ross A. Klein, Richard Lasdon, Fred Nelson, Martha Nelson, Cynthia Parsons McDaniel, Kathy Roeder, Anne Kaufman Schneider, and Darren Star.
DeVries Public Relations, New York, N.Y., who originally brought Drama Dept. and Tupperware Brands Corporation together for what became a rewarding relationship.
MiaCucina—an unrivaled source of kitchen furnishing ideas and retailer of Scavolini® kitchens, with showrooms in Aventura and Coral Gables, Florida. Many thanks to Javier Wainer and Ray Rouco for offering us their fabulous showroom for our cover photo shoot.
Fred Thompson, Book Production Resources, for shepherding us through this inaugural cookbook project with infinite patience.

PRODUCTION CREDITS:
Fred Thompson, Book Production Resources, Tampa, Florida: project management
Asia Pacific Offset, Inc., Washington, D.C. and Hong Kong: printing and binding
Becky Luigart-Stayner, Sunny House Studio, Birmingham, Alabama: food and product photography
Bruce Gore, Gore Studio, Inc., Nashville, Tennessee: cover and book design
Maureen Callahan, Callahan Culinary Communications, Westminster, Colorado: food consultant, introduction text, test kitchen director
Steven P. Widoff, Steven P. Widoff Photography, Tampa, Florida: cover photography
Polly Linthicum, Alpharetta, Georgia: proofreader
Mary Ann Laurens, Alpharetta, Georgia: indexer